Samuel Adams

Son of Liberty, Father of Revolution

OXFORD
PORTRAITS

Samuel Adams

Son of Liberty, Father of Revolution

Benjamin H. Irvin

OXFORD
UNIVERSITY PRESS

In memory of Anita Shafer Goodstein, William R. Kenan
Professor of History, the University of the South, 1963–94

OXFORD
UNIVERSITY PRESS

Oxford New York
Auckland Bangkok Buenos Aires Cape Town Chennai
Dar es Salaam Delhi Florence Hong Kong Istanbul Karachi Kolkata
Kuala Lumpur Madrid Melbourne Mexico City Mumbai Nairobi
São Paulo Shanghai Singapore Taipei Tokyo Toronto

and an associated company in
Berlin

Copyright © 2002 by Benjamin H. Irvin
Published by Oxford University Press, Inc.
198 Madison Avenue, New York, New York 10016
www.oup.com

Oxford is a registered trademark of Oxford University Press

Design: Greg Wozney
Layout: Alexis Siroc

Library of Congress Cataloging-in-Publication Data
Irvin, Benjamin.
Samuel Adams / Benjamin Irvin.
p. cm.–(Oxford portraits)
Summary: Examines the life of Samuel Adams, a hero of the American Revolution
who is credited by some with having fired the first shot at Lexington Green, the
"shot heard 'round the world." Includes bibliographical references and index.
ISBN 978-0-19-5132250
ISBN 0-19-513225-4 (alk. paper)
1. Adams, Samuel, 1722–1803—Juvenile literature. 2. Politicians—United
States—Biography—Juvenile literature. 3. United States. Declaration of
Independence—Signers—Biography—Juvenile literature. 4. United States—
History—Revolution, 1775–1783—Biography—Juvenile literature. [1. Adams,
Samuel, 1722–1803. 2. Politicians. 3. United States—History—Revolution,
1775–1783.] I. Title. II. Series.
E302.6.A2 I79 2002
973.3'092—dc21

2002004283

9 8 7 6 5 4 3

Printed in the United States of America on acid-free paper

On the cover: Portrait of Samuel Adams by John Singleton Copley, 1772

CONTENTS

PROLOGUE:
THE ELUSIVE
SAM ADAMS

"In meditating the matter of that address, I often asked myself, Is this exactly in the spirit of the patriarch Samuel Adams? Will he approve of it?"

—Thomas Jefferson

Midnight, April 19, 1775. Under cover of night, 850 British troops have landed their small boats in Cambridge, Massachusetts. Commanded by Lieutenant Colonel Francis Smith, the troops have rowed across the Charles River from Boston, where they are regularly stationed. Now, at Smith's direction, they begin to assemble as silently as possible. These soldiers, who have been handpicked from among the most trustworthy in all of General Gage's army, nervously await their command. Clearly this is not just an ordinary drill. No, these men have been selected for a mission of singular importance, a mission for which General Gage himself has handed down the orders. The soldiers, Redcoats as they are popularly known, are to march to the small town of Concord and seize the artillery and gunpowder stored there. Along the way, they are to stop near Lexington and—according to American spies—arrest the leaders of the American rebellion, Samuel Adams and John Hancock.

Meanwhile, as the British soldiers stamp the river water from their boots, Boston silversmith Paul Revere, astride a horse named Brown Beauty, gallops into Lexington. Two hours earlier, Revere, too, had rowed across the Charles, but not before ordering that two lanterns be lit in the

steeple of the Old North Church. By this prearranged signal, Revere's accomplices would know that the Redcoats
are coming by sea. In the hours that have passed, Revere
has ridden through the countryside, dodged British scouts,
and warned his fellow New Englanders that the Redcoats
are on the march. But he has not yet accomplished his primary purpose: alerting his compatriots, Adams and Hancock,
of the impending danger. Once Revere reaches Lexington,
he guides his horse directly to the home of the Reverend
Jonas Clarke, where the two leaders have been hiding for
weeks. He bangs on the door with a fervor that might wake
the whole town, and out of a bedroom window pop the
sleepy heads of Adams and Hancock.

The two Patriot leaders receive Revere's warning with
a great deal of excitement, and they deliberate for some
time as to what action they should take. They know that
the Redcoats are after the military stores in Concord. They
know, too, that while they sit debating, the local militia—
the Minutemen, as they will later come to be known—have
been rousted from their slumber and will soon gather to
defend their liberty. Perhaps most significantly, Adams and
Hancock know that a battle is likely, a battle that will push
the colonists one step closer to war, and one step closer to
the possibility of independence from Great Britain. How
they long to join in the fight!

Fortunately, cooler heads prevail. As Revere and Reverend
Clarke are well aware, Adams and Hancock are too important to the American cause to risk death or capture at
Lexington Green. They convince the two Patriots to flee
the town so as to escape the British troops; the men gather
their belongings, bid farewell to their friends, and disappear
into the countryside. Later that morning, as they rode on to
safety, they heard behind them in the distance the shots fired
at Lexington. As the Patriot minister and historian William
Gordon would later write, Adams turned to Hancock and
exclaimed, "O! What a glorious morning this is!"

John Adams lived in the shadow of his more famous cousin Samuel until he attended the Continental Congress. There, his legal thinking earned the praise of America's leading citizens.

Adams would not be captured that morning, thanks to the conspiratorial hospitality of Reverend Clarke, the horseback heroics of Paul Revere and his fellow midnight riders, and the loyalty of numerous Patriots who kept his whereabouts a secret. But just as he eluded General Gage, so too has Adams eluded historians. Indeed, despite numerous biographies written about the Patriot leader, Adams remains something of a mystery. At best, his life seems full of contradictions. The man who was born into a family of relatively high rank lived a humble, at times almost impoverished life. The man who could barely manage his own house brilliantly managed the Massachusetts House of Representatives. The man who fomented the Revolution resisted the Constitution. The man who spearheaded resistance to the English government staunchly opposed resistance to the United States government.

Adams has also largely eluded our popular imagination. When Americans think about the Revolution, they think first of men like George Washington or Thomas Jefferson. Few great monuments have been built in Adams's honor, certainly nothing with the grandeur of the Washington Monument or the stirring simplicity of the Jefferson Memorial. And yet Jefferson himself thought of Adams as "truly the *Man of the Revolution*." Why has Adams so confounded would-be captors? Why has he faded in our memory of America's Founding Fathers?

To some extent, Adams himself is to blame. During the War for Independence, before an American victory was certain, leaders such as Samuel Adams performed their Revolutionary deeds with knowledge that if they lost the war, the British would surely execute them for treason. For this reason, Adams destroyed many of the letters and documents in his possession. His second cousin, John Adams, remembered Samuel furiously at work with a pair of scissors. When John asked why he was cutting all of his papers to pieces, Samuel explained that neither he nor any of his co-conspirators would ever be hanged as a result of his failure to destroy incriminating evidence.

Adams's obscurity results from other factors as well. As with most heroes of the Revolution, many myths accumulated around Adams. According to one legend, Adams could be seen as early as 1769 walking the streets of Boston urging the people to take arms against the British army. Adams has even been credited with firing the first shot at Lexington Green, the so-called "Shot Heard 'Round the World!" Stories such as these distort the historical record, blurring our vision of the real Samuel Adams.

But perhaps the most significant reason that Adams eludes us is rooted in certain elements of his personality. Adams devoted himself passionately to his country and its cause, and in so doing, he led a very public life. In addition to many other posts, Adams served as a representative in the

Massachusetts General Court, as a delegate to the Provincial and Continental Congresses, and as lieutenant governor and governor of Massachusetts. So fully did Adams devote himself to his civic responsibilities that they in large part overwhelmed his private life. One contemporary described Adams as a man who "eats little, drinks little, sleeps little, [but] thinks much, and is most decisive and indefatigable." In fact, it seems that Adams may have purposefully hidden behind his public image. About private matters he was typically guarded and quiet, so much so that another man who knew him complained that Adams was always "too secret to be loved by his friends."

This criticism, though, was perhaps rendered with undue severity, for if Adams led a secret life, it was not because he was cold or crotchety. Rather, it was because Adams was a modest man, a devout Puritan who harbored disdain for pride and the pursuit of fame. He derived satisfaction not from his own success, but from working for the cause he believed to be just. As Samuel once explained to his wife, Elizabeth, "It is an unspeakable consolation to an actor upon the public stage, when, after the most careful retrospect, he can satisfy himself that he has had in his view no private or selfish considerations, but has ever been guided by the pure motive of serving his country." Given these sentiments, it may be that Adams would be happy to know that he has not received his share of the historical limelight. He was always content to do his good deeds quietly.

This book attempts to do what General Gage could not: capture Samuel Adams. Like all people, Adams was a complex individual. He was a product not only of his thoughts and actions, but also of his family, his religion, and his country. Raised in a household that paid close attention to Boston political affairs, Adams quickly developed his own opinions about government. He dedicated his life to public service, but not in pursuit of fame or fortune. Rather, Adams was a man of the people; a man deeply committed to liberty, and even more so to virtue; a man who gave himself tirelessly to the cause of his country.

And yet, Adams was also a man who was hopelessly out of touch with his age. He strove for simplicity in an era that yearned for extravagance. Surrounded by statesmen, he practiced the politics of a bully. Ill suited for the political climate that developed after the Revolution, Adams remained in Massachusetts rather than ascending to national office. As he grew old, Adams was bewildered and somewhat disappointed by the changing times. Indeed, the world that Adams helped to bring about, a world reconfigured by revolution, differed tremendously from the world into which he was born.

CHAPTER

SAMUEL ADAMS'S BOSTON

In 1722, the year Samuel Adams was born, Boston was a
bustling seaport community with approximately 12,000
inhabitants. Bordered on the east by the Atlantic Ocean and
on the west by the sinuous Charles River, the town was situated on a small peninsula that stretched ambitiously into
the Massachusetts Bay. Only a thin neck of land held Boston
to the mainland, and that thin neck sometimes disappeared
during high tide. Perhaps because of these unique geo-
graphical attributes, the Algonquian peoples who originally
inhabited the small peninsula called it Shawmut, or "sweet
waters." The earliest English settlers, however, referred to
the area as Trimountain, or Tremont, after the three small
hills that rose in the west.

The most prominent of these hills was Beacon Hill, and
from its crest the citizens of Boston could look out proudly
over the entire town. From the base of Beacon Hill sprawled
the Common, where animals grazed, and along the edge
of the Common could be seen the alms house, a writing
school, and a graveyard in which many of the town's early
citizens had been laid to rest. Leading away from these sites,
the streets of Boston wound their way to the harbor.

Though these streets were lined mostly with houses and a few shops, it was the steeples of the town's 11 churches that shaped the Boston landscape. Beyond these steeples could be spied tall masts of ships anchored in the Boston Harbor; beyond these lay the Atlantic Ocean. And far across this vast blue expanse, beyond the banks where fishermen cast their nets, beyond the fleets that sailed the routes of the transatlantic trade, was England. Most of Boston's citizens had never seen the shores of England, but they could feel the mother country in their history, in their ancestry, indeed, in their very blood.

The majority of Boston's inhabitants were descended from the Puritan emigrants who had journeyed to New England in the first half of the 17th century. Drawn from the eastern and southern regions of England, the Puritans ventured to America mainly for religious reasons. Strongly influenced by the wave of religious reform known as the Protestant Reformation and by theologians such as John

This view of Boston Common, from about 1770, depicts British soldiers on Beacon Hill. The hill took its name from a beacon—visible in the background just beyond John Hancock's mansion—that guided ships in Boston Harbor.

13

Calvin, the Puritans believed that the Church of England had gone astray. Anglicans, as members of the Church of England were known, relied on stained glass, incense, statues, and bells to impress upon people the holiness and power of God.

To the Puritans, such things were sheer idolatry. Religion, they argued, should be experienced in the heart and the soul, not in the trappings of a man-made chapel. Furthermore, Puritanism denied the importance of priests and bishops for individual salvation. Anglicans believed that church leaders mediated between God and the individual, that God's grace flowed through his priests to his people. Puritans, on the other hand, believed that God's grace flowed freely, and that to find the Lord, one needed only the Bible.

In the early 1600s, Archbishop Laud, the head of the Church of England, began to make life difficult for Puritan dissenters. He purged them from positions of leadership within the church, and he forbade them from worshipping elsewhere. This hostility, combined with increasing financial difficulties, convinced many Puritans to migrate from England. And so, in 1630, a small flotilla of ships, filled with Puritans under the leadership of John Winthrop, set sail for the New World.

Unlike the Pilgrims, who had landed at Plymouth Rock 10 years before, the Puritan migrants did not actually separate from the Church of England. Rather, the Puritans set out to reform the church from within, by providing a standard of the true faith. They believed that God had sent them into the wilderness of Massachusetts on a divine errand, and they hoped to build what Winthrop called a "citty upon a hill," a city for the world to behold as a model of the Christian faith. During the next two decades, as political and economic conditions worsened in England, plunging the unhappy nation into civil war, tens of thousands of settlers would join their community in what later became known as the Great Migration. One of these migrants was Henry Adams, the great-great-grandfather of Samuel Adams.

Like his neighbors, Henry Adams soon became well acquainted with the hardships of life in early Massachusetts. Though the soil was fertile, it was rocky and demanded much labor. New England winters were brutally cold; the wind whipped through the frames of the settlers' homes, and snow and ice accumulated on the roofs. Because most of these homes were built of wood, the New England settlements were particularly susceptible to fire. By 1711, no fewer than eight fires had torn through Boston's wooden buildings. Similarly, by 1721, the year before Samuel Adams's birth, the town had already suffered six outbreaks of the disfiguring and often-deadly disease known as small-pox. Yet the people of Boston carried on, striving always to prepare for themselves a place in heaven while supporting themselves and their families on earth.

Life for the New England colonists was also made try-ing by their often-hostile relations with the region's Algonquian inhabitants. Though some settlers strove to fos-ter amity and cooperation with their Algonquian neighbors, cultural differences and the competition for land and resources drove a wedge between the settlers and the Native Americans. The Algonquians recognized that these intrud-ers intended to permanently dispossess them of their land, and the result was a long history of raids, border skirmishes, and all-out warfare. In 1675, the most violent and destruc-tive of these outbreaks, King Philip's War—named after a Wampanoag sachem known as Metacom to his people but as Philip to New England authorities—destroyed 25 Puritan towns, killing more than 3,000 Indians and perhaps as many as 800 English colonists.

The decades that followed witnessed a series of battles that, though less destructive than King Philip's War, were no less violent. In 1704, for instance, an Indian war party allied with the French settlement in Quebec raided the frontier village of Deerfield, burning its homes and killing almost all of its inhabitants. Similarly, in 1708 a group of Native Americans attacked the town of Haverhill, and only a few of its residents survived. One of these survivors, a young girl named Elizabeth Rolfe, escaped the Indians who had killed her parents by hiding beneath a tub in the family's cellar. When Elizabeth grew older, she married and gave birth to a girl who one day would marry Samuel Adams.

Despite the trials of early American life, Massachusetts and the rest of the English colonies continued to grow. Free land and cheap natural resources fueled the English economy. In the southern colonies, slaves imported from Africa harvested tobacco, rice, and indigo, much of which was consumed in Europe. In New England, those colonists who settled near the coast quickly learned what the Native American inhabitants had long known: the cold waters of the Atlantic were rich with cod and clams, oysters and lobsters. New England entrepreneurs also found profit in the importation of molasses from the West Indies. They distilled this molasses into rum, which they then exported to Europe and Africa. The shipping industry also thrived, in large part because the vast forests of New England provided excellent timber for ships and boats.

The hustle and bustle of this economic activity permeated the tiny Boston peninsula. Along its wharves the wooden planks of gangways creaked beneath the weight of sailors loading and unloading their cargoes. On one street the clang of the blacksmith's hammer echoed above the rhythmic clopping of horse hooves and wagon wheels on cobblestone. Just around the corner, the pungent aromas of lye and hot wax rose from the vats of the soap and tallow makers. Here were men who worked with their hands— artisans and mechanics—men who built ships and furniture, repaired tools, tanned hides to be worked into fine leather goods, cared for livestock, and tended small gardens.

Nor was life idle for Boston's women. A few owned shops or rented rooms out to weary travelers, but most labored at home, tending family farms and gardens. Their spinning wheels turned constantly, and their looms cranked out yard after yard of cloth. These were the activities that filled Boston's streets, 100 streets in all, with such descriptive names as Milk Street, Ship Street, and Merchant's Row. And on one of these streets, in the south end of Boston not far from Bull's Wharf, lived a young couple, Deacon Samuel Adams and his wife, Mary.

Deacon Adams had been born and raised in Boston. The son of a successful ship's captain, he earned a good living making and selling malt, a grain product used to brew ale. This business brought the Deacon sufficient income for him to buy a small but attractive house with an orchard and a garden, and a few slaves to help produce his malt. He and Mary were devoted Puritans, and in their spare time they both actively participated in their church. Mary's widowed father had remarried into the family of well-known ministers Increase and Cotton Mather, and the Deacon earned his title (which was also his nickname) for his service to the Old South congregation. Together the two made a comfortable home, but it was also a home that witnessed much pain and sorrow. In their years of marriage, Mary gave birth to 12 children. Of those 12, nine died during childbirth or in infancy. Of the three who survived, one was a boy named Samuel, after his father.

In his youth, Samuel spent his days like most other children of Boston. He helped his mother with her household chores and assisted his father in the making of malt. In his spare time, he probably played at Fort Hill or sat on the nearby wharves, marveling at the tall ships that sailed in and out of the harbor.

Yet if young Samuel Adams worked and played like other children, his upbringing was not altogether like that of his peers. The reason was that his father was not like other men.

This 1743 panorama of Boston Harbor shows the town's many church steeples reaching to the heavens to receive the blessings of Providence. A thriving seaport community, Boston's wharves stretched into the bay to receive the bounties of the transatlantic trade.

In addition to his work as a maltster and his service to the church, the elder Adams was very active in local politics. For many years he served as a justice of the peace, hearing the small lawsuits of his neighbors. He also organized a political club with his friend Elisha Cooke, a fierce politician who was well respected among the Boston townspeople. Known as the Caucus Club, this organization consisted mostly of working men; in fact, the club may have taken its name from the many caulkers, or ship repairmen, who filled its ranks. The Caucus Club met regularly to discuss upcoming issues such as what position the town should adopt on various political matters, or who should serve in the town's political offices. Having reached a consensus, the members of the club would then cast their votes together at the next town meeting. In this way, Deacon Adams's Caucus Club had a powerful voice in Boston politics.

Over time, the Caucus Club became the backbone of a political faction known as the "popular" party. This loosely knit party, which would later be known as the Whig party, was typically led by native Bostonians whose primary concern was the welfare of the common people of Massachusetts. The popular party stood in opposition to the royal governor, who was appointed by the king, and the governor's "court" party. The court party, sometimes known as the Tory party, consisted of many royal officials, most of whom were born and educated in England. These appointees usually worshipped in the Church of England, and they aspired to become members of the English aristocracy.

They knew little about the people of Massachusetts, and often cared less. In addition to royal officials, many well-to-do merchants, whose political interests lay in the defense of their wealth, also belonged to the court party. In the decades that preceded the Revolution, these popular and court factions fought over the issue of the governor's salary, which was determined by the Massachusetts House of Representatives; they fought over economic matters; and they fought over the selection of the governor's council. Most importantly, they fought for the political support of the voters of Massachusetts.

Deacon Adams joined in these political battles, and as a result of his connections with the Caucus Club and the popular party, he spent many nights entertaining his fellow political activists. Men like Elisha Cooke visited his home to complain about the governor, to debate what should be done about town finances, and to outline their political strategies. At their feet played young Sam Adams. Though he may not have understood all the fine details, he heard them talk of the government, of the rights of the colonists, and of the days of the old charter, revoked by King Charles II in 1684, under which the citizens of Massachusetts had been able to elect their own governor. From his earliest years, Samuel Adams was steeped in the Puritan history and the provincial politics of his hometown.

Samuel's parents had high ambitions for their son. Mary taught Samuel to read and write, and at the age of six he successfully passed the test for admission to the South Grammar School by reading verses from the King James Bible. At the grammar school, Adams studied diligently under the supervision of schoolmaster John Lovell. Like most of the schoolteachers of his era, Lovell was a strict preceptor. He demanded that his students approach their Greek and Roman texts with discipline and dedication, for in these ancient works could be found a wealth of poetry, philosophy, and history. Only through rigorous study, Lovell believed, could a young boy stake his claim to the erudition of a well-bred Englishman.

As an incentive for his students, Lovell kept on his desk a "short stubbed, greasy-looking" rod. Sometimes he dipped this rod in sugar candy and licked it clean, but more often it was used to serve a dish less sweet. If a student was insolent, lazy, or rude, Lovell would punish him with two stinging raps upon his open hand. Fortunately for young Samuel Adams, there is no evidence that he ever provoked Lovell's ire. Indeed, his mother's tutelage had prepared him well, and it appears that Samuel grew to love the pursuit of knowledge. In the margin of one of his textbooks Adams scribbled a proverb: "The value of learning exceeds riches."

As a result of his hard work, Adams performed well in grammar school. At age 14, he became the first member of his family to attend Harvard College. In those days, the young men who attended Harvard were ranked according to the social status of their fathers. A student's rank determined where he walked in academic processions and where he sat during prayers and at student assemblies. Class rank, however, was not decided on the basis of personal wealth, but rather on the basis of prestige in the community.

In lieu of cash, Samuel's father had to pay for his son's tuition with flour, but because the elder Adams served as a justice of the peace, young Samuel was placed sixth in his class. By contrast, his second cousin John Adams, the future President of the United States, later entered Harvard ranked fourteenth. Decades later, the revolution that Samuel and John helped bring about would reshape American society according to principles of egalitarianism. The trustees of Harvard agreed with the Declaration of Independence that all men are created equal, and they abolished their ranking system.

At Harvard, Adams continued to read classical Greek and Latin texts. He also studied Hebrew, to prepare for the ministry. Mary and Deacon Adams hoped that their son would one day join the clergy, and the piety he demonstrated from an early age encouraged this dream. Parental pressure was not the only force pushing Samuel toward the pulpit. While he was at Harvard, a wave of religious reform swept over New England. For decades, economic development, immigration, and generational change had all contributed to a decline in religious fervor. Some ministers observed that their congregations seemed to have lost their zeal, if not their faith.

In the mid-1730s, an impassioned minister named Jonathan Edwards determined to wake his Northampton congregation from its spiritual slumber. Preaching fiery sermons such as his famous "Sinners in the Hands of an Angry God," Edwards sparked a series of revivals, now known as the Great Awakening, that spread throughout the colonies. In Northampton, as well as in Boston and Cambridge, young and old people alike began to renew their religious commitments, recalling the devoutness of their Puritan ancestors. Samuel Adams, too, embraced the old Puritan faith and committed himself to a life of virtue and simplicity.

Still, this faith was not enough to steer him in the direction of the ministry. Like his father, Samuel's real passion was politics. His reading of Greek and Roman historians awakened his zeal for liberty and republican government, and for the virtue that safeguarded both. In addition to the classics, the masters of Harvard taught Adams the history of modern England. Fewer than 50 years before Adams's birth the Glorious Revolution had reshaped Britain's government and constitution, securing the rights of Parliament against the throne.

With this revolution came a new era in political thought. Whig theorists, those who celebrated the Glorious Revolution and the new rights of Parliament, championed principles such as popular sovereignty and the separation of powers. They argued that political powers—such as the power to tax or the power to raise an army—ultimately derived from the people. Rather than vesting all such powers in a monarch, who could easily be corrupted, these theorists thought it safer to divide the powers of government among king, lords, and commons. Adams studied these ideas, and he pored over the writings of James Harrington,

Algernon Sidney, John Trenchard, Thomas Gordon, and other political thinkers who espoused the virtue of a land-owning citizenry and decried the vices of wealth and privilege. But none had a greater influence on Adams's thought than the writings of John Locke.

In 1690 Locke published *Two Treatises of Government*. The second of these, "An Essay concerning the true original, extent and end of civil Government," provided the blueprint for much of the political and constitutional thought of the 18th century. Locke explained that government represented a social contract into which citizens entered voluntarily. The purpose of government was to protect the rights and property of citizens, and in exchange for that protection, the people pledged their loyalty to government and submission to law.

```
      T W O  320.L
   T R E A T I S E S
   2334   O F  H 88
 GOVERNMENT:
        In the Former,
 The falſe Principles and Foundation of
 Sir ROBERT FILMER,
   And his FOLLOWERS,
    Are Detected and Overthrown.
      The Latter, is an
 E  S  S  A  Y
        Concerning the
    True Original, Extent, and End of
 CIVIL GOVERNMENT.
   By JOHN LOCKE Eſq;
      The FIFTH EDITION.
 Quod ſi nihil cum potentiore juris humani relinquitur inopi,
 at ego ad deos vindices humanæ ſuperbiæ confugiam : Et
 precabor ut iras ſuas vertant in eos, quibus non ſuæ res,
 non alienæ ſatis ſint : quorum ſævitiam non mors noxiorum
 exſatiet : Placari nequeant, niſi hauriendum ſanguinem
 laniandaque viſcera noſtra præbuerimus. Liv. l. 9. c. 1.

      L O N D O N:
 Printed for A. BETTESWORTH in Pater-Noſter-Row,
  J. PEMBERTON in Fleetſtreet, and E. SYMON in
  Cornhill. M,DCC.XXVIII.
```

Locke argued if a government failed to fulfill its end of the bargain, that is, if government violated the property or rights of its subjects, then the people had a right to revolt. Locke's treatises radically challenged the idea that the king had a divine right to rule, and they would later provide the ideological justification for the Declaration of Independence. Young Samuel Adams found himself engrossed in Locke's writings, which helped to explain the political opinions of men such as his father, Elisha Cooke, and their friends in the Caucus Club. And at an early age Adams came to realize that his destiny lay in politics.

John Locke was an English philosopher and political thinker who believed that governments were formed to protect the rights and property of individuals. His Two Treatises of Government *influenced the drafters of the Declaration of Independence.*

RAISED FOR REBELLION

Samuel Adams's passion for politics was ignited in college by his reading of classical historians and of Locke and other liberal writers. But this passion was further fueled by events that transpired just after Adams graduated from Harvard. In the early 1740s, Samuel's father, Deacon Adams, became embroiled in the most torrid political controversy of the early 18th century. This controversy erupted over a financial scheme known as the land bank. Developed by Deacon Adams and his political allies, the land bank was a plan to rescue the colony from economic disaster. In 1733, Parliament had passed the Molasses Act, which increased the tax on the key ingredient in rum, New England's most valuable export. The Molasses Act devastated not only the liquor manufacturers but also the shipbuilders and longshoremen whose income depended upon the trade of that commodity. Worsening the crisis was the growing scarcity of specie, that is, gold and silver, in the colony. Local merchants had been using this "hard" money to pay their debts to London creditors, but little specie had been coming back into the colony.

To alleviate the effects of this financial crisis, Deacon Adams and his colleagues resurrected the land bank, an age-old system of providing "soft," or paper, money. The plan was relatively simple. Adams and the other charter members of the bank, almost 400 landowners from around the bay, each pledged up to £2,000 of their own money. These pledges were secured by mortgages on the members' real estate properties, hence the name "land bank." In exchange for their pledges, bank members were issued paper bills that they could circulate around the colony. After 10 years who-ever then held the bills could redeem them for hard currency, but in no case would a bank member be responsible for more than the value of his original pledge. In March 1740, the land bank opened for business, with Deacon Adams serving on its board of directors.

The land bank was wildly popular with the working people of Boston. Within a few months more than 1,000 people had borrowed money and begun to repay their debts. Yet while popular with the working classes, the land bank was bitterly detested by Boston's leading merchants. The paper bills were of little worth to merchants, who could not pass them along to their creditors in England where the bills had no value. And even within the colony, the bills' value could rise and fall unpredictably. To Boston's wealthy merchants, the bills represented a cheap and unfair way for the townspeople to escape their debts.

In most matters of politics, these merchants followed the court faction. They had powerful connections in England, and they typically lent their political support to the royal governor, Jonathan Belcher. For this reason, Belcher was quick to respond to their complaints about the land bank. Even though such organizations were legal—as recently as 1734 the Board of Trade had authorized a New Hampshire land bank—Belcher immediately ordered the House of Representatives to investigate the matter. But many members of the House had pledged money to the bank, backed by their own property, and the people of Boston depended upon the paper currency. Not surprisingly, the House refused to comply with Belcher's order. Outraged by this resistance, Belcher issued a proclamation forbidding any individual who held a royal commission from associating with the bank. Rather than abandon the bank, Deacon Adams promptly resigned his commission as a justice of the peace.

Because it provided economic relief to so many citizens, there was little that Belcher alone could do to quash the land bank. Certainly the Massachusetts Assembly would not take any action against it. Cornered, the governor appealed to Parliament. In 1741, Parliament passed "An Act for restraining and preventing several unwarrantable schemes and undertakings in his Majesty's Colonies and Plantations in America." This act effectively outlawed the land bank. Even worse, it imposed severe penalties on the men who had organized it. Parliament ordered that the directors of the bank were individually liable for *all* of the bills it had issued. Deacon Adams and his fellow directors, who had joined the bank under the assumption that each would be responsible for only the £2,000 he had pledged, now found themselves responsible for all of the bank's obligations. As if this were not enough, the law held that if the directors failed to pay these debts immediately in gold or silver, the courts could hold them liable for three times the amount owed. Deacon Adams would spend the rest of his life in court defending his property against land bank creditors.

Governor Belcher defeated the land bank, but at great political expense. Recognizing that Belcher had alienated much of the House and created an enormous rift in Massachusetts politics, royal authorities removed him from office in 1741. But by that time much of the damage had been done. Backed by the colony's leading merchants, Belcher and his royalist supporters had made enemies of the popular party and the yeomen, artisans, and laborers that it represented. Parliament, too, had earned the scorn of the people. Justice, so it seemed, was a luxury for the rich, and the much-heralded rights of Englishmen were mere trifles. Belcher's successor as governor, William Shirley, was left with the unenviable task of restoring faith in the royal government.

Young Samuel Adams was barely 20 years old when Governor Belcher crushed the land bank. He studied political events as they unfolded, he observed the governor's indifference to the welfare of his subjects, and he suffered from financial insecurity as his father scrambled to protect his property from the courts. The land bank crisis left a deep impression on Samuel. He came to recognize that, in the eyes of the English government, Massachusetts and her sister colonies were still little more than frontier outposts whose sole purpose was to fill the king's coffers. Adams grew resentful of royal officials who meddled in the lives of the colonists, and like his father he yearned for the day when the people of Massachusetts would once again govern themselves, as they had before Charles II revoked the colony's charter in 1684.

Adams soon found an opportunity to vent these frustrations. In 1743, he returned to Harvard to obtain a master's degree. As a prerequisite for graduation, master's candidates were at that time required to demonstrate their learning by posing a philosophical question and defending an answer to it. Adams posed the question "Whether it be lawful to resist the Supreme Magistrate, if the Commonwealth cannot be otherwise preserved?" He answered in the affirmative. Summoning all of the wisdom he had gathered from John Locke, Adams argued that citizens could disobey their king in order to protect the social compact. More than three decades before the Declaration of Independence was written—indeed, in the very year that Thomas Jefferson was born—Adams had begun to contemplate opposition to the mother country. But not even in the impertinence of his youth could Adams have foreseen the conflict to come.

In the meantime, Adams had a more practical matter on his mind: he needed to earn a living. He could not run for political office, as he might have wished, because he had not yet developed the necessary social connections or proved himself worthy to the people of Boston. In 1740 Adams took a job working as a clerk in the countinghouse of a local merchant, Thomas Cushing.

Like Deacon Adams, Cushing was a prominent figure in the popular faction. Young Samuel might have relished the prospect of working with the statesman, but Cushing was looking for a talented clerk, not a political protégé. To Cushing's disappointment, Adams was a failure at business. He simply did not care for making money. In fact, he felt a Puritanical disdain for luxury and the accumulation of wealth. Many years later he would explain, "I glory in being what the World calls, a poor Man. If my Mind has ever been tinctured with Envy, the Rich and the Great have not been its objects."

It was fortunate that Adams felt this way, because his career would be marked by a series of financial failures. After only a few months working as a clerk, Adams was sent home. According to Cushing, Adams spent too much time thinking about politics and not enough time thinking about his ledgers. His father agreed to help him get back on his feet, and he generously gave Samuel £1,000 to support himself until he could find another job. Again young Adams demonstrated his ineptitude with finances. He loaned the money to a friend, hoping to earn some interest, but the friend squandered the money and never repaid his debt. Samuel fell back on the only option available to him. He went to work for his father, making malt that the people of Boston would ferment into vinegar and ale.

The elder Samuel Adams may well have welcomed his son's assistance. Ever since the collapse of the land bank, Deacon Adams's energies had been consumed with protecting his property from lawsuits. Fortunately, the Massachusetts House of Representatives placed limits on the amount of damages that land bank plaintiffs—people who owned the now-worthless land bank notes—could obtain. But the elder Adams still found himself hauled into court by his

Founded in 1636, Harvard College was situated in Cambridge, just across the Charles River from Boston. Samuel Adams graduated from Harvard in 1740 and returned for a master's degree in 1743. Deacon Adams paid Samuel's tuition with flour.

enemies. The voters of Boston, on the other hand, rewarded Deacon Adams for leading the land bank fight. In June 1746, he was elected to the Massachusetts House of Representatives. In 1747, the members of the House nominated him for a seat on the governor's council, the highest position of political authority not appointed by the king. Governor Shirley, however, recognized that Adams wielded tremendous influence over the popular party, and he knew better than to entrust him with so much power. Shirley summarily vetoed Adams's nomination as soon as it was made.

Though his bid for councilor had been thwarted, Deacon Adams had risen to new political heights. As a member of the legislature, with strong ties to the Caucus Club, Adams was well situated to control the popular party. Ironically, however, political events in Europe limited the influence of Adams's power. In 1740, the death of Charles VI, the Holy Roman Emperor, triggered the War of Austrian Succession. Slowly, each of the powers of Europe was dragged into the fighting.

In 1745, the conflict crossed the Atlantic when French and Indian forces raided English settlements in Maine. Known as King George's War, this conflict crippled the popular party.

Because the residents of New England depended upon the mother country to protect them from the French and Indians of Canada, and because they benefited from the money and supplies that England sent in their defense, the war evoked an outpouring of loyalty. Especially after the land bank turmoil had subsided, it seemed unpatriotic to pick political fights with the royal governor. Even the more disaffected members of the House recognized that the time had come to patch over old political differences. The popular party, whose political power depended upon its opposition to the governor, would have to bide its time.

Even though the frontier conflict inaugurated a brief era of political harmony, the British government still found ways to enrage the people of Boston. Two crises arose out of the British administration of King George's War. The first and more incendiary of these crises was known as the Knowles Riot. In November 1747, British naval commodore Charles Knowles dropped anchor in Boston Harbor. Knowles had sailed into the bay from Isle Royal, now known as Cape Breton, at the northern tip of Nova Scotia, where he had commanded a squadron in the battle against the French fleet. He returned to Boston because desertions and the casualties of war had left him short of manpower.

To alleviate this shortage, Knowles intended to rely on an ancient naval practice known as impressment. Under this practice, which was permitted by the unwritten English constitution, British officers would send large gangs of armed sailors roaming through port cities in search of able bodies. These press-gangs were authorized to kidnap young men, using force if necessary, and bring them aboard ship, where they would be made to work as sailors. Malnutrition, scurvy, seasickness, flogging, shipwreck, drowning, and injury or death in battle were just a few of the hardships with which an impressed sailor might have to contend. For this reason, the sight of a man-of-war sailing into port struck fear in the hearts of Boston citizens. Sailors, dockworkers, and young tradesman of all sorts immediately fled into the countryside, and business came to a grinding halt

Embittered by what they saw as the kidnapping of their sons, brothers, and friends, and frustrated by the disruption of their livelihood, the residents of Boston decided to fight back against the practice of impressment. For only a few months earlier, the House of Representatives had appointed Adams to a committee whose task was to devise a way to protect Massachusetts's inhabitants from impressment by the royal navy.

When Commodore Knowles's press-gangs stepped ashore, they were met by a number of citizens, armed and ready to defend themselves. A large crowd soon gathered around Governor Shirley's mansion, where the commodore and other officers were believed to be hiding. Shirley ordered the local militia to disperse the crowd, but the militiamen, whose sympathies were with the townspeople, refused to answer the muster. Shirley escaped to Castle William, located on an island in Boston Harbor, and the violence began to escalate. The crowd, which had already seized a naval officer, assaulted a sheriff and locked his deputy in the stocks. Only when Commodore Knowles agreed to release the seamen did the crowd disperse. The impressment crisis passed, but the people of Massachusetts once again saw that their interests were at odds with those of the mother country.

This lesson was reinforced by the second crisis to arise out of King George's War. The trouble arose when the Treaty of Aix-la-Chapelle, which brought an end to the conflict, was announced in 1748. As a condition of peace, the English agreed to return to France all possessions captured during the war. To the colonists' dismay and disbelief, this included Fort Louisbourg. Situated on Isle Royal, Fort Louisbourg looked out over the Gulf of St. Lawrence. Whoever controlled the fort also controlled the St. Lawrence River and all of the water traffic to the French city of Quebec.

Early in the war, as the fighting began to intensify, the citizens of New England determined to capture the fort. In

April 1745, a fighting force of 4,000 volunteers, sailing in a fleet of 90 vessels, set out for Isle Royal. Under the command of William Pepperell, a Maine merchant with little military experience but great courage, the New Englanders invaded the island and launched a bold assault against the fort. In July, the news reached Boston that Louisbourg had been taken. The peal of church bells and cannon fire announced the good news to the countryside.

Now, just three years after that heroic victory, the English government had given the fort back to the French. The people of Massachusetts were outraged. Not only was the capture of Louisbourg a tremendous strategic accomplishment, but this military feat had symbolic meaning as well. The sons of New England had sacrificed their lives in the name of the king, and they had proved to themselves and the world that they could fight, and defeat, one of the greatest powers of Europe. Who were the treaty negotiators to deny them the fruits of their victory? The British government could not, of course, undo the treaty, but it did attempt to appease the people of Boston. The king made William Pepperell a baronet, and Parliament agreed to reimburse the province for the cost of the expedition. Still, the residents of New England felt cheated.

As was his nature, young Samuel Adams followed these events closely. He listened to his father talk of the debates in the House of Representatives. Politics consumed him, and he continued to develop his own opinions. In 1747, Adams found an outlet for his political energies. He and several friends, young men whom he knew from town and from his days at Harvard, organized a club that met to discuss politics. This group met regularly and shared their insights about the theories of the great Whig writers, as well as their thoughts on local political affairs.

These conversations were warm and very satisfying to Adams and the others, but still the group longed to accomplish more. They wanted to make a difference in Boston politics, and so, in 1748, the club began to publish its own newspaper, the *Independent Advertiser.* Members of the club agreed to take turns submitting articles for the *Advertiser,* and they swore themselves to secrecy. As was the custom for newspaper writers and pamphleteers, authors would remain anonymous, perhaps so as not to incur reprisals from those politicians that they attacked. The *Advertiser* was short-lived; it lasted a little more than a year. But in its brief life span the paper gave its readers a Whig perspective on politics. The *Advertiser* also enabled its contributors to cultivate their writing skills and to develop the ideas that would guide them through the coming decades.

One theme that resounded through the pages of Adams's paper was virtue. The *Advertiser* chastised the citizens of Boston for having lost sight of the pious simplicity of their Puritan ancestors. The paper lamented that the people had become absorbed with material possessions and the accumulation of riches. In the process they had become slaves to their wealth and, all too often, had abandoned their Puritan faith.

The *Advertiser*'s call for virtue was part of a longstanding tradition that had many sources. Puritan ministers of the 17th century had been famous for preaching jeremiads, long sermons that urged their congregations to give up their wicked ways and turn again to the piety of previous generations. Virtue also had a classical component, and once again Adams's education came in handy. The Roman statesman Cato had implored his fellow citizens to forgo worldly pleasures and resume the honest labor upon which Rome had been built. Samuel Adams always kept such an exhortation on the tip of his tongue, and in later years he would be remembered as the Cato of the American Revolution.

The call for virtue held further significance in the context of English history. Whig political thinkers argued that the English government had grown corrupt. Nepotism, the act of appointing one's relatives to office without regard to talent or ability, was a regular practice of British officials.

During King George's War in 1745, Maine merchant William Pepperell led a force of 4,000 fighting New Englanders in a successful assault on the French fort of Louisbourg. As this song conveys, the people of Massachusetts celebrated "New England Bravery" and felt great pride for having defeated a European power.

New England Bravery

Being a full and true Account of the taking of the City of *Louisbourg*, by the *New-England* Forces under the Command of the gallant General *Pepperell*, on the 17th of *June*, 1745. Tune of, *Chivey-Chace.*

Come all *New-England's* gallant Lads,
and lend to me an Ear,
And of your Brethren's mighty Acts
I will in short declare.
Brave Pep'rell with three Thousand Men,
(perhaps some hundreds more)
Did land the very first of *May*,
upon *Cape Breton* Shore:
And tho' opposed by *Morepang*
with full two hundred Men,
A handful of our gallant Lads
did drive them back again.
Some few were taken Prisoners,
and many kill'd out-right,
Which taught the *French* at *Louisbourg*
New England Men can fight.
The *Monsieurs* all astonished
to see our Armament,
Were griev'd to see that they must be
within Stone Walls all pent.
In haste they call in to their Aid
the Men upon the Isle,
Forgetting their own Poverty,
(such Things would make one smile)
But what is vastly more absurd
Than any thing like this,
They quitted the *Grand Battery*,
the Glory of the Place.
Of which our *English* Lads did take
Possession quietly,
And with the Guns did ever since
the Enemy annoy.
They also did with mighty Toil
their Batteries erect,
Against the Town and Citidel,
which play'd with good Effect.
They sent such Showers of Bombs and Balls
as made the *Frenchmen* quake,
And sputter out such Words as these,
Those Dogs the Place will take.
Our Men did also batter down
the West Gate and the Wall,
And made therein so large a Breach
that to the *French* they'd call,
Come out, Jack Frenchman, *come to us,
and drink a Bowl of Punch,*

Jack Frenchman cries, *you* English *Dogs,
come, here's a pretty Wench.*
But by and by they change their Tones,
and offer Terms of Peace,
Which if consented to they would
surrender up the Place.
(For they were so severely maul'd
by Cannon Shot and Shells,
That they no Place of Safety found
on Platforms or in Cells.)
Their Island Battery likewise,
on which they much depended,
Was so annoyed by our Men
it could not be defended.
For they did wisely plant some Guns
upon the Light House Point,
And also one good Mortar-Piece,
which put them out of Joint.
Our Lads they fir'd so furiously
into that Island Fort,
The Soldiers jump'd into the Sea,
which made our Men good Sport.
Our Gen'ral upon this Success
did send *Monsieurs* Word,
If they would not give up the Place,
He'd put them to the Sword.
And now not daring to withstand
the Force of all our Bands,
They gave up all their Fortresses
into our *English* Hands.
With Beat of Drums and Colours spread
the Seventeenth of *June*,
Our gallant Army marched in,
'bout Twelve o'Clock at Noon.
The Gentlemen and Ladies too
they did caress our Men,
For having them delivered
from worse than Lion's Den.
They all are to be sent to *France*,
with all the Islanders,
Which needs must ease our Countrymen
of many Cares and Fears.
And all the Men are strictly bound
(that is as we do hear)
Not to bear Arms against King George,
at least for one whole Year.

Sold at the Heart and Crown in Cornhill, Boston.

Positions of authority often were sold to the highest bidder, and extortion was commonplace. The *Advertiser* made similar accusations against the Shirley administration. In June 1748, for example, Adams wrote that

> When Vanity, Luxury, and Prodigality are in Fashion, the
> Desire of Riches must necessarily increase in Proportion
> to them... *Not only Matters of Favour, but of Justice too,
> will be expos'd to Sale;* and no Way will be open to

Honours or Magistracies, *but by paying largely for them.*
He that gets an Office by these Means, will not execute
it *gratis*: He thinks he may sell what he has bought; and
would not have entere'd by corrupt Ways, if he had not
intended to deal corruptly...And the Corruption thus
beginning in the Head, must necessarily diffuse it self
into the *Members* of the Commonwealth.

The *Advertiser* also sounded a personal note for Adams. It
argued that the governor's power to veto council nominations should be revoked. Two years earlier, Governor Shirley
had vetoed Deacon Adams's nomination, and Samuel still
held a grudge. The *Advertiser* doled out so many verbal lashes
that members of the court party began to refer to the paper's
anonymous authors as the Whipping Post Club. Flogging
royal officials kept Samuel preoccupied and provided a nice
mental reprieve from the physical demands of making malt.
But in 1748, a tragedy befell the Adams household, putting
an abrupt end to Samuel's pursuit of publishing. Deacon
Adams died at the age of 59. Samuel was deeply saddened.
He had lost his father, his friend, and his role model. In the
Advertiser he published a moving obituary and prayer:

> Last week died and was decently interred the remains of
> *Samuel Adams,* Esq.; a gentleman who sustained many
> public offices among us, and for some time past repre-
> sented this town in the General Assembly. He was one
> who well understood and rightly pursued the civil and
> religious interests of this people; a true New England
> Man; an honest Patriot. Help, Lord, for such wise and
> godly men cease, and such faithful members fail from
> among the sons of New England.

Deacon Adams had been a strong mentor, and Samuel
resolved to fulfill his father's legacy. He had come of age
during a period of tremendous political tumult, and he had
been raised by one of the most important figures in Boston's
popular party. Now he had inherited his father's mantle,
and it would not be long before Samuel would take the lead
of that party himself.

TIS NOT IN MORTALS TO COMMAND SUCCESS

Upon Deacon Adams's death, responsibility for the family malt business naturally fell upon Samuel's shoulders. His sister, Mary, and his brother, Joseph, had grown and moved out of the house, and his aging mother could scarcely run the business by herself. It must have been an overwhelming time in Adams's life. At 26 years of age he was very much a man, and yet he had lived many of those years as an apprentice to his father. While the elder Adams watched over the malt operation, Samuel had little incentive to develop his own business skills. He enjoyed relative freedom from the burdens of adulthood, and he possessed enough leisure time to pursue his passion for politics. Now all of that had changed. Adams suddenly found himself struggling to manage a household.

Perhaps it was no coincidence that one year later Samuel proposed marriage to his lifelong acquaintance, Elizabeth Checkley. Elizabeth's family was well known to the people of Boston. Her mother had survived the notorious Haverhill massacre of 1708, and her father, the Reverend Samuel Checkley, served as the pastor of the New South Church. Just around the corner from Adams's home, the New South had been built in 1716. Samuel's father, a deacon of the Old South Church, helped found the New South, and he encouraged Reverend Checkley to lead the congregation. Young Samuel Adams regularly attended services at the New South, and it may have been there that he first caught Elizabeth's attention. He was fond of singing hymns, and was known by fellow churchgoers for his "exquisite ear for music, and a charming voice."

Samuel and Elizabeth were married by her father on October 17, 1749. In Elizabeth, Samuel found an excellent helpmate. She kept house industriously, and in later years Samuel would write that her "exact economy" was admired by his family as well as her own. Elizabeth's virtues could not, however, save the couple's marriage from tragedy. Within a year after their wedding, Elizabeth gave birth to a boy named Samuel, who died in infancy. A year later Elizabeth gave birth to another boy, again named Samuel. Much to the family's joy, this second son survived. But in 1753 a third son, named Joseph after Samuel's brother, died just two days after his birth. Elizabeth and Samuel's first daughter, Mary, was born in 1753. Named after Samuel's mother, Mary survived for four promise-filled months, but she too died an infant. The Adamses' losses were great. Nine of Samuel Adams's own siblings died young; he was one of only three who lived to adulthood. The death of his siblings and of so many of his own children may have caused Samuel to despair of his family's ill fortune. Not for three more years did he and Elizabeth have another child.

In the meantime, Samuel continued to work at the malt business, and he pursued a series of minor official positions. One of his earliest appointments was that of town scavenger, a job that required him to collect rubbish from the streets of Boston. From that ignoble station Adams worked his way up to inspector of chimneys, a small but important job in a town that had been repeatedly destroyed by fire. He served on a committee to inspect local schools, he briefly maintained records for the town market, and he also held a position as collector of the liquor excise tax. At times, his climb up the political ladder felt exceedingly slow, but in each of these posts he earned a little more of the public confidence. These additional responsibilities also kept Adams distracted from the pain of so many personal losses.

Elizabeth and Samuel's perseverance was once again challenged in the summer of 1756. In July, Elizabeth bore a second daughter, named Hannah. Haunted by the memories of the children they had lost, it was with great trepidation that Elizabeth and Samuel surrendered themselves to their hopes for Hannah's future. Fortunately, their hopes, and their prayers, were fulfilled: Hannah survived infancy. Their daughter brought great happiness to the young couple, and they might have thought their sorrows ended. But one year later Elizabeth delivered a stillborn son. Of her six children only two had survived. The emotional and physical toll on Elizabeth was tremendous, and on July 25, 1758, just 19 days after her last child was stillborn, Elizabeth passed away.

A mournful widower, Samuel remembered his wife as a sincere friend and faithful wife. In the family Bible he wrote that Elizabeth "ran her Christian race with remarkable steadiness and finished in triumph. She left two small children. God grant they may inherit her graces."

Samuel barely had time to grieve for Elizabeth's passing before he was confronted with another personal crisis. In 1758 the General Court, as the House of Representatives was also known, ordered Sheriff Stephen Greenleaf to auction the Adams's property in order to pay off Deacon Adams's old land bank debts. Seventeen years had passed since Governor Belcher had shut down the land bank, yet the piddling claims of the Deacon's creditors had come back to torment his grief-stricken son. Samuel began to feel that his world was collapsing around him. Having lost four children and a beloved wife, he found himself left alone to raise young Samuel and Hannah.

THE Dwelling-Houfe, Malt-Houfe, and other Buildings, with the Garden and Land adjoining, and the Wharf, Dock and Flatts before the fame, being Part of the Eftate of the late *Samuel Adams*, Efq; deceas'd, and is fituate near Bull-Wharf, at the lower End of Summer-Street in *Bofton* aforefaid, the faid Eftate being taken by Warrant or Execution under the Hands and Seals of the Honourable Commiffioners for the more fpeedy finifhing the *Land-Bank* or *Manufactory-Scheme.*

The Plan of the Ground and the Terms of Payment may be known by enquiring of
Stephen Greenleaf.

To pay off Deacon Adams's old debts, Sheriff Stephen Greenleaf threatened to auction off the home that Samuel had inherited from his father. Samuel Adams proceeded to take out his own ad, threatening to prosecute anyone who trespassed on his estate.

As he struggled to endure these hardships, he recalled the afflictions of Job, and he strove to emulate the patient suffering of that Old Testament patriarch. But now, as the sheriff threatened to take the roof from over his children's heads, Samuel's patience reached its limits. When the Boston Newsletter announced the pending sale of Adams's "Dwelling House, Malt-House, and other Buildings, with the Garden and Lands adjoining," Samuel responded by taking out an ad of his own. Addressed to Greenleaf, Adams's message warned that he would "prosecute to the law any person whomsoever who shall trespass upon that Estate." It may be that this warning convinced Sheriff Greenleaf not to auction the property. Or, as one of his enemies later reported, it may be that Adams threatened the sheriff with physical harm. Whatever the case, Greenleaf abandoned his efforts to sell the estate, and Adams was able to keep his home.

So great were Adams's personal trials that he seems to have hardly noticed the war going on around him. In 1754, American soldiers commanded in part by Major George Washington of Virginia clashed with French and Indian forces in western Pennsylvania. For the fourth time in 50 years, the major powers of Europe battled on North American soil. This final conflict, known in America as the

French and Indian War and in Europe as the Seven Years' War, would ultimately result in the surrender of Canada by the French to the English. In the meantime, the war again eased tensions between the court and popular parties. By flooding the New England colonies with money and supplies, the British government effectively bought the loyalty of her North American citizens. Massachusetts' newly appointed governor, Thomas Pownall, further enhanced political relations by catering to the popular party. He succeeded in smoothing over differences with what had traditionally been the governor's rival faction.

However, as had been the case during King George's War, the political harmony brought about by the French and Indian War soon turned to discord. The reason was that many American merchants earned enormous sums during the war by illegally trading goods in the French West Indies. Devastated by the war's economic impact, the small French settlements in the Caribbean posed no military threat to the New England colonies. For this reason, the merchants of Massachusetts felt few qualms about smuggling goods to the islands, even though they were, in fact, trading with the enemy. Enforcement of the Navigation Acts was traditionally very loose, and customs officials, if they could not be bribed, could just as easily be harassed into cooperation. Smuggling became a lucrative business.

In order to halt this illegal trade, the royal government began to crack down on Boston merchants. In the spring of 1761, British authorities seized four merchant ships for customs violations. Each of the vessels and its cargo was sold at auction, causing exorbitant losses for its owners. Such penalties were extremely harsh, and Boston merchants were frantic. The loss of a ship and its freight could easily bankrupt an overextended ship owner. So, to protect their profits, the merchants launched a series of courtroom attacks against the customs officials who had been hounding their illicit trade. These legal battles centered upon the lawfulness of special

search warrants known as writs of assistance, which empow-
ered royal customs agents to inspect the holdings of a ship or
warehouse even if there was no evidence to suggest that a
crime had been committed. Because they granted unlimited
power of inspection to the meddlesome officials, these warrants
rankled Boston merchants, who insisted that they violated
English constitutional liberties. But King George II had personally authorized the Superior Court of Massachusetts to
issue the writs, and it seemed that there was little the merchants could do to fight them.

In need of assistance, the merchants turned to a young
lawyer from Barnstable County named James Otis, Jr. Otis
had known Samuel Adams at Harvard, and like Adams, he
descended from a powerful political family. Both of their
fathers served in the House of Representatives. But unlike
Deacon Adams, Colonel James Otis, Sr., belonged to the
court party, and had been counted among the closest friends
of Massachusetts' governors. In 1760, however, the new governor, Francis Bernard, made the Otis family his enemies.

This dramatic estrangement took place when Bernard
overlooked the colonel for an appointment to the Superior
Court. Years earlier, Governor Shirley had promised to give
the next open seat on the court to Colonel Otis, but none
became available during either Shirley's administration or
that of his successor, Pownall. When a judgeship finally did
come available, the younger Otis expected that Shirley's old
promise would be kept. He immediately began to lobby
Governor Bernard on his father's behalf. To be on the safe
side, the younger Otis also appealed to the lieutenant governor, Thomas Hutchinson, whom he confidently assumed
would recommend Colonel Otis for the judgeship. To the
Otises' dismay, Bernard gave the judicial appointment not
to the colonel, but rather to his supposed ally, Hutchinson.

The elder Otis felt deeply betrayed, and from his seat in
the House of Representatives he abandoned the royal faction. The younger Otis also felt affronted by Bernard's

choice, but he reserved his fury for Thomas Hutchinson. Otis believed not only that Hutchinson had lied when he offered to support his father, but, more detestably, that Hutchinson had used his position as lieutenant governor to shore up the judicial appointment for himself. Otis huffily resigned his position as the King's Advocate General in the Vice-Admiralty Court, and he moved his practice to Boston, where he swore to take his revenge against the lieutenant governor.

Hutchinson was an easy target for Otis's spite. The son of a wealthy merchant, Hutchinson was well-bred and popular. He was also exceedingly handsome; even his enemies were forced to admit that Hutchinson's good looks had "captivated half the pretty Ladies in the colony." And his affluence and refinement had further captivated "more than half the pretty Gentlemen." But if Hutchinson represented all that was elegant and genteel, he also represented all that was rotten in the British Empire. Though American by birth, Hutchinson longed to feel a part of the British aristocracy. He believed that most people were unfit to rule themselves, and that government was better entrusted to the privileged few. His own political career embodied this principle. Before his appointment on the Superior Court, he simultaneously held no fewer than four political positions, each of which added a healthy income to his riches. Now he held the highest judicial post in the colony, even though he had never received a day of legal training. This was precisely the sort of plural office holding that Whig thinkers on both sides of the Atlantic despised.

The controversy over the writs of assistance gave James Otis the chance to wreak his revenge against Hutchinson. For months Otis brooded over the merchants' plight, vainly searching for a court decision or statute that might invalidate the writs. Then, late in 1760, news arrived from England that George II had died. Otis got the break he had been waiting for. Under English law, all official papers bearing the king's seal would soon have to be renewed by

George III, including the order authorizing the writs of assistance. This technicality provided an opportunity for Otis to question the writs in court.

In one of the greatest ironies of colonial Massachusetts politics, the legality of the writs came to be determined by the Superior Court, presided over by none other than Chief Justice Thomas Hutchinson. Otis found himself arguing before his sworn enemy, who now sat on the very bench that should have belonged to his father. Otis could not afford to squander

this opportunity. All of Boston's leading men attended the hearing, including the colony's finest attorneys. Though the law was against him, Otis argued poignantly in defense of the colonists' rights. For several hours, Otis's oratory burned like "a flame of fire." No act of Parliament, he proclaimed, could bind an English citizen if it were contrary to natural law. His eloquence was persuasive, and his audience was deeply moved. John Adams later recounted that "American independence was then and there born...Every man of a crowded audience appeared to me to go away, as I did, ready to take arms against writs of assistance." Against such public sentiment, all that Hutchinson could do was backpedal. Only by delaying his decision, and waiting for the public's passion to subside, was Hutchinson ultimately able to uphold the writs.

Despite losing the case, Otis won a powerful moral victory. In the next election, the people of Boston rewarded

An ardent supporter of royal authority, Thomas Hutchinson held many high offices in Massachusetts politics. The Whig newspaper, the Boston Gazette, *mockingly observed that Hutchinson's handsome face had "captivated half the pretty Ladies in the colony" and his genteel manners had captivated "more than half the pretty Gentlemen."*

him with a seat in the House of Representatives, and he quickly breathed new life into the popular party. Upon moving to Boston, Otis seized the opportunity to renew his old acquaintance with Samuel Adams. Adams had been keeping his hands busy and his wit sharp by writing against the royal party in the Boston newspapers, and Otis recognized him as a formidable ally. Perhaps even more appealing to Otis than Adams's pen was their mutual disdain for Thomas Hutchinson. In the 1740s Hutchinson had gone out of his way to destroy Deacon Adams's land bank. Now Adams watched gleefully as Hutchinson made another political enemy. For the next several years, Otis and Adams joined forces to harass the lieutenant governor. While Adams wrote newspaper articles lambasting corruption in the royal government, Otis pushed a bill through the House reducing Hutchinson's salary. He also lobbied to remove Hutchinson from at least one of his multiple positions. Although this latter effort failed, Otis and Adams drew much public attention to Hutchinson's plural office holding, badly embarrassing their foe.

The fallout over the writs of assistance was of greater significance, though, than the fulfillment of Otis's personal vendetta. Rather, the controversy resulted in a major realignment of Boston's political parties. Previously, the merchants of New England sided with the governor and his royal party. They opposed the land bank, for instance, and had struggled to keep Massachusetts under a system of hard currency. But the crisis over the writs caused a schism in the royal party. The merchants made fortunes from their smuggling, and they resented British attempts to interfere with their trade. The battle over the writs pushed many merchants into the happy embrace of the popular opposition.

One such merchant was John Hancock. Hancock had inherited tremendous wealth from his uncle, and Adams realized that Hancock's money could one day come in handy for the Whig party. Together, Adams, Otis, and Hancock collaborated in a series of endeavors designed to weaken the royal faction. In 1762, for instance, the three men organized a society of Puritan ministers, funded no doubt out of Hancock's purse, to preach to the Indians of New England. Their concern was not so much with converting their Native American neighbors as it was with stemming the missionary efforts of Anglican priests, who were thought to be allied with the English government.

Evangelizing was not Adams's strong suit, however, nor did it earn him a living. His malt business had long since foundered, and in order to eke out his existence, Adams accepted a position as town tax collector. He performed this job without much rigor, for the people of Boston were not well situated to pay their taxes. In 1764, an outbreak of smallpox debilitated the town, causing many residents to close their businesses. Having suffered through money problems of his own, Adams was not personally inclined to push his fellow citizens into financial turmoil. Like his father, who had crusaded for the land bank to ease his neighbors' debts, Adams was a friend to the poor. But Adams was motivated by more than pure altruism. By overlooking a tax payment here or there, he earned the affection and political allegiance of Boston's working people.

In part because of his popularity as a tax collector and in part because of his close relationship with James Otis, Adams's influence began to be felt more forcefully in several of Boston's many political arenas. He shaped backroom politics through his leadership of the Caucus Club, the political association of working men that his father helped establish. Together with the Merchants' Society, which was now under Otis's sway, the Caucus Club controlled most of the town's affairs. Given that Otis and Adams wielded such authority, it is hardly surprising that they loomed over the town meeting itself. And it was in the town meeting that Adams took his first major political step.

Adams's opportunity arose in the spring of 1764 when word arrived from London that George Grenville, chancellor of the exchequer, had introduced in Parliament a new plan for raising money for the British Empire. The Chancellor's financial reforms became necessary because the long and expensive Seven Years' War had drained British coffers. Most government officials agreed with Grenville that the colonists should bear the burden of new taxation. It was in defense of the colonies, after all, that Britain had accumulated her wartime debt. So, Grenville proposed a three-pence-per-gallon tax on molasses imported into the colonies to make rum. Known as the Sugar Act, this tax actually represented a reduction of the tax imposed by the Molasses Act of 1733. Massachusetts merchants, though, avoided paying the older tax by smuggling molasses into the colonies. Now, as British customs officials tightened the screws on illegal smugglers, it seemed that the new three-pence tax would have to be paid.

The people of Boston would not stand idle in the face of this new tax. At the next town meeting they appointed a committee to prepare instructions for their delegates in the House of Representatives. Instructing delegates was nothing new to the Boston populace; the practice was central to the province's representative government. But because they were written in opposition to the Sugar Act, these instructions were of heightened importance. By entrusting Adams to chair the drafting committee, the townspeople signified that his years of work as an elected official, his many articles in the local newspapers, and his countless hours of behind-the-scenes politicking had finally paid off.

If to most Bostonians the Sugar Act represented a bothersome financial burden, to a lover of liberty such as Adams it represented a gross infringement on the colonists' rights as English citizens. Adams was alarmed because the Sugar Act represented an extreme departure from English tax policy. Parliament had levied taxes against commodities before, even against molasses. But the purpose of taxation had always been to regulate the trade of those commodities. Never had a tax been imposed specifically for the purpose of raising revenue. Even more alarming was Grenville's suggestion that the Sugar Act was only the beginning of a broad new scheme of taxation. As the Preamble to the Sugar Act proclaimed, "[N]ew provisions and regulations should be established for improving the revenue of this Kingdom."

Thus when Adams picked up his pen to write the instructions, he did so with tremendous passion. "[W]hat still heightens our apprehensions," he wrote, "is, that these unexpected proceedings may be preparatory to more extensive taxations upon us. If our trade may be taxed, why not our lands? Why not the produce of our lands & every thing we possess or make use of?"

Adams then put forth a principle of just government that would later serve as a cornerstone for the War of Independence. "If taxes are laid upon us in any shape without our having legal representation where they are laid," he queried, "are we not reduced from the character of subjects to the miserable state of slaves?" Long before "No taxation without representation!" became a rallying cry for American Patriots, Adams was arguing that such taxation was both unconstitutional and unfair. Adams based his argument on a powerful blend of English constitutional principles and natural law. He urged Boston's representatives to fight for the Sugar Act's repeal, and he encouraged them to develop relationships with other colonies so "that their weight may be added to that of this province."

Boston's instructions to the House was the first public document that Adams composed, but even this early work displayed his radicalism. In 1764, few colonists could yet echo Adams's outspokenness against Parliament or second his call for cooperation among colonies. As a result, Adams was extremely disappointed to see the Massachusetts government succumb to the Sugar Act. Outside of Boston the citizens of New England were almost completely indifferent to the tax. The brunt of the tax's burden would be borne by the merchants who imported molasses; why, then, should the farmers of western Massachusetts quarrel with the mother country? Time, though, would prove Adams a prophet, and his warnings about increased taxation would ring in the ears of those who had doubted him.

In the meantime, Samuel Adams once again sought consolation in his family life. In the early winter of 1764, Adams remarried. Almost a decade had passed since his first wife had died, and the intervening years had been a time of personal and professional struggle. His malt business had fallen apart, his home had been besieged by creditors, and amidst all of these tribulations he had labored tirelessly to scrape together an existence for his family. With 40 years upon his head—in an era when most men did not live past 60 and his own father had died at 59—Adams was beginning to feel the effects of old age. His muscular body had begun to weaken, and his light blue eyes now strained to read.

Though the instructions he had written on behalf of the Boston town meeting bade well for the future of his political career, his yearning for public service had been rewarded only with the thankless position of tax collector. But Adams was never one to dwell on life's difficulties. In later years he would repeatedly write, "Tis not in Mortals to command Success," and he took this advice to heart. Even in periods of difficulty Adams managed to find reason in life to celebrate. His son, Samuel, was nearing manhood, and young Hannah soon would reach adolescence. Indeed, Adams's life already seemed to be reaching a turning point, and the happiness brought by his second marriage confirmed that his misfortunes might just reverse themselves.

Samuel's new wife, also named Elizabeth, was the daughter of Francis Wells, a wealthy English merchant who had migrated to Boston in 1723. Only 24 years old, Elizabeth was very much Adams's junior. Reputed to be a punctilious housekeeper, Elizabeth made a tremendous impact on the home of the beleaguered widower. Samuel and his two children would have been enough to keep Elizabeth's hands full, but Samuel also owned a large, shaggy Newfoundland dog named Queue, who kept his mistress busy. Shortly after their marriage, a friend of Elizabeth's presented her with a slave girl, perhaps to assist the young wife with her chores. But Samuel Adams would have nothing to do with it. Though his father had owned slaves, and he had grown up with slaves in his home, Samuel decided that he no longer could in good conscience keep slaves of his own. Had he not, after all, just warned the people of Boston against becoming the slaves of British tyranny? So when Surry, as the slave girl was known, came to the Adamses' home, she was emancipated first, and she lived with the family as a free woman until her death.

Though Elizabeth's housekeeping ability was an asset to Samuel Adams, he benefited more from her ardent support of his political career. Such support was necessary, for not long after their marriage Samuel's career took an unexpected leap. Just as Adams had predicted, Chancellor Grenville introduced another plan of taxation, much more devious than the first.

Enacted in March 1765, the Stamp Act was a tax on the conduct of business. Every document that the colonists used, be it a newspaper, a legal document, or even a deck of playing cards, would have to bear a costly royal stamp. Unlike the provisions of the Sugar Act, which only encumbered those merchants trading in molasses, the Stamp Act placed a burden on every colonist, even those who lived in the countryside. Anticipating colonial opposition, Grenville delayed the effective date until the first of November. Eight months would be more than enough time for American tempers to cool, or so Grenville and his allies thought. Adams thought otherwise. Eight months would be more than enough time for the people of New England to prepare their resistance.

American colonists were enraged by the Stamp Act, a new scheme of taxation authorized by Parliament in 1765. The act required colonists to purchase stamps for use on legal documents, newspapers, pamphlets, and even playing cards.

SAM THE PUBLICAN AND THE STAMP ACT RIOTS

When in the spring of 1765 word of the Stamp Act's passage reached Samuel Adams, he wondered what he could do to stave off the dreaded duties. As head of the Caucus Club and as a leading voice in Boston town meetings, he could not sit idly by. At the very least he would once again write Boston's instructions to the town's representatives in the General Assembly. But Adams's experience with the writs of assistance and the Sugar Act had taught him that there was little the colonial legislatures could do to reverse an act of the British government. To make matters worse, Governor Bernard and Lieutenant Governor Hutchinson had been working for some time to shore up support for the court party in the House of Representatives, and for a brief time the Whigs looked like they might falter. Lacking any legal means of resisting Parliament, many of Adams's neighbors began to accept the Stamp Act as a painful but inevitable burden.

However, just as Adams's outlook began to dim, news arrived from Virginia that invigorated the New Englanders. On May 30 and 31, the House of Burgesses, which was Virginia's equivalent of the Massachusetts House of Representatives, met to debate the Stamp Act. This assembly, whose ranks included such Patriots as Patrick Henry and George Washington, boldly protested against Parliament's authority to tax the colonies. Only the government of Virginia, declared the burgesses, had the power to tax Virginians, and any attempt by any other government to tax the people of that colony was unlawful.

The Virginia Resolves, as these declarations came to be known, sent tremors through the American countryside. Their meaning was clear: the Stamp Act was invalid and Parliament had no right to tax the colonists. Some decried the resolves as treason, but others saw in them a true patriotic spirit. In Massachusetts, the leaders of the popular party were embarrassed that Virginia had outpaced them in the fight against British taxation. Oxenbridge Thatcher, Boston's representative in the House and a friend of Samuel Adams, exclaimed that unlike Massachusetts's timid leaders, the Virginians "are men! They are noble spirits! It kills me to think of the lethargy and stupidity that prevails here."

Adams was delighted to hear the Virginia legislature echoing his arguments against taxation without representation, but certainly he shared Thatcher's frustration with the popular movement. He recognized, though, that the Virginians' courageous stand would help to rekindle a spirit of resistance. Most importantly, the Virginians had shown Boston's leaders a way out of their dilemma. The colonial legislatures could not, it was true, repeal the Stamp Act, but they could declare it unlawful, and the people could then justifiably resist its application.

The cogs of the Massachusetts popular party began to turn again. Samuel Adams knew that before any fight could be waged, he first would have to win the hearts of the citizens of New England. And so, once again, Adams picked up his pen. The pages of the *Boston Gazette* poured forth article after article against the Stamp Act. "It is inconceivable," Governor Bernard complained, how the Virginia

Resolves "have roused up the Boston Politicians, & been the Occasion of a fresh inundation of factious & insolent pieces in the popular newspaper."

While their newspaper editorials incited the Boston populace, Adams, Otis, and their cohorts worked to devise a strategy to prevent the enforcement of the Stamp Act. Two decades earlier, Deacon Adams had helped lead the fight against Commodore Knowles's impressment gangs by rallying the people to defend their liberties. Now Otis and Adams planned to resort to similar tactics. Their first step was to identify those friends and neighbors whose patriotism could be counted on. In searching for allies, Adams made the most of all of his personal relations. For years he had cultivated friendships with men of high standing, such as Otis, Hancock, and Dr. Joseph Warren. John Adams later wrote that his cousin

> made it his constant rule to watch the rise of every brilliant genius, to seek his acquaintance, to court his friendship, to cultivate his natural feelings in favor of his native country, to warn him against the hostile designs of Great Britain and to fix his affections and reflections on the side of his native country.

Adams relied on his connections with these "geniuses." And, of course, he relied on the relationships he developed in the Caucus Club with fellow tradesmen and artisans such as the silversmith Paul Revere.

Adams also worked outside the Caucus Club to expand his acquaintance with the common people of Boston. He knew that in a pinch he could call into service those friends whose tax obligations he had overlooked. He could also call on several men for whom he had found jobs in Hancock's warehouses. But not all of Adams's support came from people who owed him favors. Adams had strong ties with the town's sailors, journeymen, and apprentices. Adams spent much of his time among Boston's working classes, and because he had for many years labored as a maltster, they

GREEN DRAGON TAVERN

Where we meet to Plan the Consignment of few Shiploads of Tea. Dec 16 1773

Jan Johnson Water Street Boston - Mass. 1773

Samuel Adams earned the nickname Publican for spending hours in pubs conversing with the working people of Boston. At the Green Dragon Tavern, a regular meeting place for the Sons of Liberty, Adams and other patriots hatched a plan to destroy British tea.

considered him one of their own. He also was a frequent patron of alehouses such as the Green Dragon Tavern where working men would meet at the end of the day.

Adams spent so much time in these establishments that his Tory enemies began to call him Sam the Publican. This nickname took a double meaning from *publicus,* the Latin root for "of the people," and pubs, the places where Adams could often be found mingling with Boston's working-class men.

It may have been in the back room of one of these smoke-filled pubs that Adams and his associates laid out plans for the organization of a new, secret society known as the Loyal Nine. Named for the number of its members, the Loyal Nine was formed for the specific purpose of thwarting the Stamp Act. Neither Samuel Adams nor James Otis actually belonged to the Loyal Nine; as prominent political figures they could not afford to be too closely connected to this clandestine group of men. But both Adams and Otis had very strong ties to the Loyal Nine. Henry Bass, a cousin of Samuel Adams, was one of its members, along with

Thomas Chase, a member of the Caucus Club, and Benjamin Edes, publisher of the *Boston Gazette* in which Adams's and Otis's articles had regularly appeared. These were men who knew the streets of Boston, and who knew how to keep a secret. All of them belonged to the town's working classes, and like Samuel Adams, they were intimately acquainted with the young men of Boston.

The young men of Boston, in turn, were a rowdy, rough-and-tumble lot, well suited to perform the Loyal Nine's dirty work. These toughs, mostly teenaged apprentices and boys, belonged to two rival gangs, one from the South End and the other from the North End of Boston. Silent and orderly during most of the year, these gangs erupted into violence every November 5. Known in the colonies as Pope Day, November 5 marked the anniversary of the foiling of the Gunpowder Plot of 1605, in which Guy Fawkes conspired to blow up the House of Lords. Fawkes, a Catholic, also intended to kill King James I in retaliation for James's anti-Catholic laws, but his plot was discovered and he was eventually hanged for treason.

Every year in celebration of Fawkes's capture, Boston's South and North End gangs would construct elaborate effigies of the pope, who had allegedly masterminded Fawkes's conspiracy; the devil, who had whispered the plot in the pope's ear; and "King" James III, the "old pretender" who claimed to be an heir to the English throne. After parading these effigies on wagons through the streets of Boston the two gangs would then meet on Fort Hill where they would fight a bloody brawl, each gang struggling to capture the other's pope. While fists flew and bones crunched, mild-mannered Bostonians locked their doors. So vicious were these Pope Day riots that in 1764, the year preceding the Stamp Act, a small boy was killed after falling under the wheel of a parading wagon, and yet the rumble continued.

The "captain," or leader of the South End gang, was a young shoemaker named Ebenezer McIntosh. Like his counterpart in the North End gang, McIntosh had close relations with both the boys he commanded and with the town's older and more reputable tradesmen. In the small town of Boston, McIntosh had grown up knowing most of his peers. He was also connected to other young men through the town's division of labor. Typically, the boys of Boston worked as apprentices and were responsible to the artisans they served. In turn, these tradesmen formed alliances such as the Caucus Club with local mechanics, and were also connected through their business relations with the town's shopkeepers and merchants.

This pecking order was to some extent replicated in ritual events such as town meetings and militia exercises. At the time of the Stamp Act, the men of Boston were thus tied to one another in a loose hierarchical system that could be easily mobilized. As Samuel Adams was well aware, the members of the Loyal Nine could, when the time was ripe, rally a small army of apprentices, sailors, and young boys to do the bidding of the Patriot leaders.

The time ripened on August 14, 1765. When the sun rose over Boston that morning it cast a strange shadow on the Common. High in the branches of a large elm—which would come to be known as the Liberty Tree—hung an effigy of Andrew Oliver, the man whom Chancellor Grenville had appointed to distribute the royal stamps. Also hanging from the tree was a large black boot, out of which peered the horned head of the devil. The boot represented the Earl of Bute, an advisor to King George who was wrongly believed to have concocted the Stamp Act. The display suggested that the devil, Lord Bute, and Andrew Oliver had colluded to oppress the people of Massachusetts. With this display, the Loyal Nine made an ominous first strike.

Governor Bernard and Lieutenant Governor Hutchinson were at a loss as to what should be done about the effigy. On the one hand it seemed like a harmless prank, best to be ignored. On the other, the effigy represented a direct

A VIEW OF the YEAR 1765.

Paul Revere's engraving A View of the Year 1765 *portrays American opposition to the Stamp Act. At left, colonists, guided by Minerva, the Roman goddess of wisdom, attack tyranny—represented by a dragon. The dragon is aided by the flying demons, Spite and Envy. At right, John Huske, a supporter of the Stamp Act, hangs in effigy from the Liberty Tree.*

affront against a royal official; the dignity of the Crown dictated that Oliver's likeness should be removed. After consulting with the governor's council, Hutchinson ordered Sheriff Stephen Greenleaf to tear down the effigy. But when Greenleaf and his deputies arrived at the tree they were met by a large number of men who warned that anyone who attempted to remove the effigy would find himself hanging alongside it. And so the effigy stayed until later in the day when several hundred men gathered at the Liberty Tree. Many of the men were young Pope Day rioters, but also, as the Boston Tories later reported, some were merchants and artisans disguised in workingmen's clothes. In command of this army was none other than Ebenezer McIntosh, the captain of the South End gang.

From the Liberty Tree, McIntosh and his men marched the effigy through the streets of Boston to the chamber where Bernard and his council were convened. "Liberty, property, and no stamps!" they cried, and then with three loud "huzzahs" the crowd set out for Kilby Street. There they arrived at a new office building, still under construction, that belonged to Andrew Oliver himself. The crowd believed that Oliver intended to use the building as his Stamp Office, and so with the efficiency of a demolition crew, the crowd tore it to the ground. The throng then proceeded to Oliver's home. Some of the men hurled rocks through Oliver's windows. They then beheaded the effigy so that Oliver would know what his fate would be if he chose to distribute the stamps. The rioters then moved on to Fort Hill, near Samuel Adams's home, where they built a bonfire from the planks and boards they had torn from Oliver's office.

By now it had grown late in the evening. Governor Bernard feared the tumult would not subside and he ordered the colonel of his militia to drum up his troops. The drummer was unavailable, the colonel laconically replied, because he and most of the militiamen had joined the crowd. Seeing that nothing could be done, Governor Bernard fled to Castle William, just as his predecessor Governor Shirley had done during the impressment riots twenty years before.

Bernard's lieutenant governor, Thomas Hutchinson, was able to muster a little more courage than that. Along with Sheriff Greenleaf, Hutchinson marched to Oliver's house, intending to disperse the crowd. But before he could even make the order, he was chased off by a horde of men brandishing brickbats and throwing rocks. The crowd could not be stopped. Perhaps recognizing that it ruled the town, the crowd returned to Oliver's house to torment the would-be stamp distributor. They kicked down his garden fences, ripped shutters from the house, and broke down his doors. Once inside they destroyed furniture and might have torn down the whole house as they had done Oliver's office. Finally, though, a neighbor managed to convince the crowd that Oliver had fled to the countryside, and around midnight the crowd went home.

Whether or not Samuel Adams was in the streets that night, it is doubtful that he got much rest. Not in two decades had he or his fellow townspeople witnessed a protest of such magnitude, and the excitement must have burned in his heart. The protest had its desired effect. Andrew Oliver returned from hiding to discover that his house had been ransacked, and he immediately announced that he had had enough; he would not serve as distributor of the stamps. Certainly no one else would be foolish enough to volunteer for the position, and it now seemed that the Stamp Act could not be enforced in Massachusetts. Even Governor Bernard was sadly forced to admit, "For my part I am entirely at the Mercy of the Mob." Patriot leaders such as Otis, Adams, and the Loyal Nine rejoiced at their accomplishment, and soon thereafter they began calling themselves the Sons of Liberty. Similar organizations sprang up throughout the colonies and many cities followed Boston's lead in rioting against the Stamp Act.

However, Adams soon learned an important lesson of caution in his dealings with the crowd. On August 15, just one night after Oliver's home had been so badly damaged, another group of young men rallied on Fort Hill. This crowd marched to Thomas Hutchinson's home, perhaps because he had attempted to interfere the night before, and began beating on his doors. Fortunately a neighbor convinced the crowd to leave. But a few days later, on August 26, the dark summer sky was once again illuminated by bonfires on King Street. On this night two mobs arose. The first proceeded to the home of William Story, an enemy of Boston merchants. This crowd broke into Story's home and destroyed his legal documents. The second mob dispatched for the home of Benjamin Hallowell, a despised customs official. Hallowell's assailants broke his windows and pulled shutters and doors from their hinges. They destroyed furniture, ripped wainscoting from the walls, and burned Hallowell's books and papers. They then plundered Hallowell's wine cellar.

The two crowds then united, and having fortified themselves on Hallowell's wine, they once again marched behind McIntosh to the home of Thomas Hutchinson. Courageously enough, Hutchinson at first vowed to stay and defend his property, but the pleas of his fearful daughter convinced him to flee. The mob showed him no mercy. For several hours the rioters systematically destroyed his home. They tore apart the woodwork, knocked out windows and doors, and broke fine furniture to pieces. They destroyed family portraits, shredded clothing, and cut down trees in Hutchinson's orchard. The crowd stole £900 and looted his silver. Finally, and perhaps most painfully for the lieutenant governor, the mob took the hand-written manuscripts of Hutchinson's own *History of the Province of Massachusetts Bay,* and scattered them through the town's muddy streets. The mob remained at Hutchinson's home, demolishing whatever it could, until daybreak finally threatened to reveal the rioters' identities.

The mood in Boston was somber the next day. No one knew for sure why the mob attacked Hutchinson's home. Some speculated that Otis ordered the attack out of revenge for the personal wrongs Hutchinson had done him. Others thought that the assault had been orchestrated by a third party who wanted certain legal documents destroyed. Still others supposed that the drunken crowd had simply escaped its leaders' control. Whatever the case, even the most ardent supporters of the popular party thought that the mob had gone too far.

Adams and his colleagues felt great distress. They never meant for the violence to get so out of hand. Though it was legal, they believed, to riot against oppressive taxation, personal assaults were not justified. Moreover, they feared that the destruction of Hutchinson's home would provoke sympathy for the lieutenant governor and damage the reputation of the Patriot cause. These leaders agreed to convene a town meeting to condemn the mob's behavior. Governor Bernard also summoned the militia to stand watch over the town. This time the militia did not refuse. Bernard was less successful, however, in having the rioters brought to justice. At the governor's request, Sheriff Greenleaf arrested Ebenezer McIntosh, who accompanied the Sheriff without resistance to the town jail. Certain Patriot organizers, perhaps even Samuel Adams, warned Greenleaf that if he did not immediately release McIntosh the militia would disband and surrender the town to the mob once again. Greenleaf had no choice but to comply.

Despite the cloud cast by the mob's excesses, the Stamp Act riots still shined brightly in the eyes of Samuel Adams. The Stamp Act duties no longer threatened to disrupt Boston business, and none of Adams's neighbors would lose their means of livelihood. Perhaps most spectacularly, Otis and Adams had pulled the popular party from the brink of submission and driven it toward new heights of resistance. Even the Massachusetts countryside, long a Tory stronghold, had joined ranks with the Whigs.

So great was his victory that Adams may have felt that he had reached the peak of his career. But fate had a larger design in store. In September, just one month after the riots, Adams's friend and colleague Oxenbridge Thatcher died prematurely of tuberculosis. Thatcher had been a zealous supporter of the popular cause and a lifelong acquaintance of the Adams family. He had also been a vocal member of the popular party in the Massachusetts House of Representatives. Upon his death, the people of Boston elected Samuel Adams to replace him. On September 27, 1765, as he took his oath of office, Adams must have thought about his father, who had held a representative's seat so many years before. He might also have reflected upon the many years of service he had given to the townspeople of Boston. At last he had reached the political pinnacle of which he had always dreamed. His education, his failed newspaper, his work in the Caucus Club: all of these endeavors had prepared him for this moment. By electing Adams to the

Just before the Stamp Act was to go into effect, William Bradford, publisher of the Pennsylvania Journal and Weekly Advertiser, *announced the "death" of his newspaper: he would quit printing rather than pay the dreaded stamp tax.*

House, the people of Boston finally rewarded him for his lifetime of effort on their behalf.

Though new to the House, Adams exerted significant power. Adams immediately took seats on several committees, and in these positions he continued to fight the political battle against the Stamp Act. He was chosen to draft the House's reply to an address by the governor and again to pen the Massachusetts Resolves of 1765. In both of these documents Adams denied Parliament's right to tax the people of New England. Just as important, Adams began to articulate the primacy of natural law over the laws of man. Using language that prefigured the Declaration of Independence, Adams wrote, "[T]he inhabitants of this Province are unalienably entitled to those essential rights in common with all men...no law of society can, consistent with the law of God and nature, divest them of those rights." By appealing to the laws of nature, Adams and his contemporary Patriots proposed the existence of a higher authority against which the acts of Parliament could be held unlawful. This principle later became one of the foremost justifications for revolution.

Meanwhile, opposition to the Stamp Act was growing throughout the colonies. Early in the summer of 1765, James

Otis had proposed, perhaps at Adams's suggestion, that representatives from the various colonies meet to discuss the Stamp Act and to formulate a unified response. In October, three delegates from Massachusetts, including Otis, departed for New York to attend what became known as the Stamp Act Congress. This was a momentous assembly. On only one prior occasion had delegates from the colonies met collectively: in 1754, when the Albany Congress convened in response to a moment of crisis preceding the French and Indian War. Now, it seemed, the Stamp Act posed as great a threat as those terrifying enemies once had. For almost two weeks the delegates debated what should be done.

Back in Boston, Samuel Adams waited anxiously to hear what course of action they would recommend. Yet he was not overly optimistic. Adams knew that few of the colonies embraced Massachusetts' radicalism. Furthermore, Governor Bernard had managed to secure the appointment of two royal sympathizers to represent Massachusetts alongside Otis. Still, Adams was not disappointed with the congress's declarations. As the Virginia and Massachusetts legislatures had earlier, the Stamp Act Congress declared that Parliament had no right to tax the people of America. The congress further proclaimed that the stamp duties "have a Tendency to subvert the Rights and Liberties of the Colonists." These, Adams recognized, were important declarations. But he also recognized that the greater significance of the Stamp Act Congress was the willingness of the colonies to work together in their fight against British tyranny.

Now that the Stamp Act had been declared null throughout the country, all that remained for Adams to do was celebrate while it went unenforced. As November 1, the date that the duties were to go into effect, drew near, Governor Bernard feared the worst. On advice of his council, Bernard ordered the militia to stand watch over the town from October 31 through November 6, one night after the annual Pope Day riots were to take place. Once again the militia refused, and once again Bernard retreated to Castle William. But to the surprise of Boston Tories, the first of November witnessed no new commotion. The Sons of Liberty did hang an effigy of Lord Grenville from the Liberty Tree, but rather than erupting into a house-breaking melee, the day's protest culminated in an orderly procession through town.

The Sons of Liberty made an even more amazing display of restraint on the fifth of November. Rather than the bloody brawls to which the people of Boston were accustomed, they were treated to a military parade. The once-rival gangs now marched shoulder to shoulder, obediently fulfilling the orders of their commander Ebenezer McIntosh, who donned full military regalia and was accompanied at the head of his corps by the colonel of the Massachusetts militia. Samuel Adams must have smiled as his troops marched by. He and other Patriot leaders celebrated the coming together of the two gangs by hosting a lavish banquet for McIntosh and his men. Many toasts were drunk, presumably on John Hancock's tab, and this grand dinner party came to be known as the Union Feast. Not only had the two gangs been united with one another, but collectively they had been united with Adams and other Patriot leaders. For the next few years, these troops would serve only at their leaders' bidding.

Boston's Stamp Act protests had almost come to an end. Even Bernard and Hutchinson acknowledged that no stamp duties would be collected. But there remained one final task for the Loyal Nine to complete. Adams and the Nine needed to keep Boston businesses in operation. Some merchants feared that their goods might be confiscated if they traded without the stamps. Such trade was, after all, prohibited by the Stamp Act. But Adams and the Nine convinced the merchants that, if the British government did not make the stamps available, then traders could not be held responsible for conducting business without them. All that was needed now was a formal declaration that no stamps would be distributed, and this could come only from Andrew Oliver.

Though Oliver had already made private assurances that he would not distribute the stamps, the Sons of Liberty insisted that he go public. On December 17, in the midst of a heavy rainstorm, Ebenezer McIntosh accompanied Oliver from his home to the Liberty Tree. There, despite the torrential downpour, some two thousand Bostonians convened to hear Oliver resign once again. Soon thereafter, the courts, the customhouses, and all the other businesses of Boston resumed their affairs, not a stamp to be found among them.

Back in England the failures of the Stamp Act were glaringly apparent. Almost all of the colonies had witnessed one form of riot or another, and it was obvious that enforcement was not worth the effort. American sympathizers in Parliament praised the colonists for their courageous fight, and many prominent London merchants expressed relief that the Stamp Act would not dampen their transatlantic trade. Lord Grenville came under heavy attack for his misguided policy, and on February 21 Parliament voted to repeal the law altogether.

Yet however willing Parliament was to recognize its mistake, it was not willing to accept the colonists' assertions that they could not be taxed. On the same day that Parliament repealed the Stamp Act it also adopted a new statute known as the Declaratory Act. This law simply declared that Parliament was in fact the supreme legislative assembly of the entire British Empire, and that it had the right to legislate for the colonies "in all cases whatsoever." In other words, Parliament would tax whomever it pleased. News of the Stamp Act's repeal was met in Boston with great celebration. So loudly did church bells peal that the New Englanders might not have heard the news of the Declaratory Act. Nor did they particularly care. They had banded together to defend themselves against British tyranny and now they had achieved victory. For Samuel Adams this was a sweet success indeed.

MOBS AND MASSACRE

The spring of 1766 was a period of personal triumph for Samuel Adams. As a recently elected member of the House, he had risen to a new level of prestige. For years Adams had listened to Reverend Samuel Checkley preach against the vanities of material reward and social standing. But now, as he walked the streets of Boston, and felt the eyes of his fellow townspeople gazing upon him with heightened respect, not even a devout old Puritan such as Adams could resist the pangs of pride. Owing much to his leadership, the popular party had been revitalized, the people of New England had been united, the several colonies had acted collectively, and, most significant, the Stamp Act had been repealed.

Adams's achievements were apparent not only to the citizens of Boston, but also to his fellow politicians. Though he had held his seat in the General Court for only a few months, he exercised tremendous sway over the popular faction. Whig leaders were well aware that Adams could mobilize the people of New England, but they also held great admiration for his strengths as a writer. As a regular contributor to Boston's radical newspaper, the *Gazette,* and as the author of important state papers such as the Massachusetts Resolves,

Adams became famous for his artful pen. Out of esteem for his strengths as a propagandist, and for his seemingly boundless political energy, the House of Representatives in May 1766 chose Adams to serve as its clerk.

Still, though, success never came easy for Samuel Adams. Not long after he had settled into his new position, Adams found himself hauled into court. Two years had passed since he had resigned his position as tax collector, but his leniency had come back to haunt him. Adams now owed the town of Boston the considerable sum of £4,000 in uncollected taxes. It may be that this new litigation was born out of New England parsimony; certainly Adams's neighbors were watchful of their wallets. But it is more likely that Adams's Tory enemies instigated the litigation for political purposes. A lawsuit coupled with the threat of bankruptcy might keep Adams busy for weeks, months, or even years. Adams's career might further suffer from the insinuation, later made by Thomas Hutchinson, that he had embezzled public funds for personal use.

Adams, however, had defended his estate before, and he was not afraid to defend it again. He also held a card up his sleeve: the attorney representing the town treasurer who filed the suit against Adams was none other than his political ally, James Otis. Not surprisingly, Adams won his case in the Court of Common Pleas, and he was for a brief time excused from his obligations. But Adams had fewer friends on the appellate bench. Reversing the trial court's decision, the appellate court ordered Adams to pay a reduced judgment of £1,463. Fortunately, though, he was granted a reprieve of several months to scrape together the money. No payment would come due until March 1768.

No payment would be made then either. Instead, Adams appeared before the Boston town meeting with a petition requesting more time to collect the taxes that were owed him. The town meeting, of course, consisted largely of the people who owed Adams taxes, and after some debate, they agreed to grant Adams another extension. This extension was hotly contested by Adams's enemies. Foster Hutchinson, the brother of Adams's arch foe, Thomas, countered with his own petition urging the town to demand immediate repayment. But Adams's friends again prevailed. One year later, in March 1769, Adams convinced the Boston town meeting to accept what limited sums he had gathered up, as well as the names of those who still had not paid their taxes. In 1772 the matter was finally put to rest when a specially appointed committee determined that Adams's remaining obligations could not be collected.

Meanwhile, the British government was also having difficulties raising funds. Ever since the Stamp Act's repeal, royal authorities had been scrambling for new sources of revenue. In 1767, Charles Townshend, the new chancellor of the exchequer, proposed a series of taxes that collectively became known as the Townshend Duties. Townshend had learned a lesson from Lord Grenville's mistakes. Rather than place a tax on the colonists' internal affairs, as Grenville's Stamp Act had done, Townshend instead proposed a tax on goods that the colonists traded overseas. Specifically, the Townshend Acts imposed duties upon commodities including glass, paper, lead, and tea.

Had the Townshend Acts stopped there, Samuel Adams might not have been able to foment any protest at all. For even though the taxes were imposed for the dubious purpose of raising revenue, they did target external trade. In this regard, the Townshend Duties were supported by a century of precedent. They functioned in much the same way, for example, as did the Molasses Act of 1733. Furthermore, unlike the Stamp Act duties, which applied evenly to the colonial population, the Townshend Duties applied primarily to the seacoast merchants who traded in dutiable goods. Adams knew that Whig sympathizers in the Massachusetts countryside would be reluctant to speak out against taxes they did not have to pay.

Fortunately for Adams, the Townshend Duties did not stop there. Chancellor Townshend recognized that American merchants traditionally avoided paying taxes by bribing customs officials or by smuggling goods into the colonies. Thousands of pounds of revenue had been lost, Townshend estimated, because merchants had illicitly escaped taxation.

To strengthen revenue enforcement, the chancellor proposed as part of his tax scheme a new agency known as the American Board of Customs. This agency would be staffed by a slew of royal officials whose job it was to search the hulls of ships coming into port for dutiable goods. Any merchant caught smuggling was subject to fines and other penalties; for some crimes the merchant's ship could even be forfeited to the Crown. As if these provisions were not odious enough, Townshend decided to post his officials where they could best keep an eye on the colonies' most active smugglers. The American Board of Customs would be headquartered in Boston.

As he had done with the Stamp Act, Adams set about to devise a strategy of resistance. Years of experience had served Adams well, and he was keenly attuned to the opinions of his countrymen. He quickly recognized that the Townshend Duties would not produce the sort of public outcry that the Stamp Act had. The people of Boston would not tolerate another series of tumultuous riots and house-breakings. Adams knew that for his strategy to succeed, it would have

After Parliament revoked the Stamp Act, Chancellor of the Exchequer Charles Townshend proposed a new series of taxes on glass, paper, lead, and tea imported by the colonists.

69

to be cautious, subtle, and ever mindful of the lengths to which Bostonians were and were not willing to go.

In the fall of 1767 Adams put his plan into action, and as was his natural inclination, he made his first move at a Boston town meeting. On October 28, Adams proposed that the merchants of Massachusetts impose a boycott on British goods. By refusing to import dutiable goods, the colonists could avoid paying taxes without breaking any laws. Furthermore, this scheme would reduce the profits earned by London exporters, spurring those exporters to protest the taxes as well. Adams's proposed boycott, which came to be known as nonimportation, thus offered a peaceable and politically tenable means of opposing the Townshend Acts.

But nonimportation represented more than that. As a young man, Adams had admonished his neighbors in the pages of his *Independent Advertiser.* Contemporary New Englanders, Adams lamented, had grown dependent upon fashion, material wealth, and worldly success. Forgotten was the spirit of their Puritan ancestors; lost was the sober simplicity of an earlier way of life. Two decades had passed since Adams's newspaper days, but his Puritan convictions had only grown stronger. Nonimportation embodied those convictions. It demanded that the people of Boston make the personal sacrifice of forgoing luxury goods to serve the common good.

Not all of the Bostonians who attended the town meeting were enthusiastic about Adams's proposal. Some worried about how Parliament might react. Others wondered whether the colonists could make do without the boycotted goods. Still others pointed out, with some justification, that merchants would not readily accede to a boycott. How could the merchants afford to lose so much profit? And how could the boycott possibly be enforced? What was to keep greedy merchants from breaking the nonimportation agreement? Adams calmly took note of these objections. He would not be worried by a few naysayers. For now it was sufficient that he had planted the seed. More significant, Adams had displayed his capacity for moderate, even passive resistance. Surely no one could now suggest that Adams was a violent radical.

Exactly one week after proposing his nonimportation scheme, Adams found another opportunity to demonstrate for the people of Boston just how mild he could be. In a case of colossally bad timing, Townshend's customs officials landed in Boston on Pope Day. Since the Union Feast two years before, the North and South End gangs had abandoned their annual riots and had allowed Pope Day to pass in relative tranquility. But even Boston's more genteel citizens recognized that by arriving on November 5 the customs officials were asking for trouble.

As tempting as these targets may have been, however, Whig leaders ordered restraint. McIntosh and his men lined the streets that day, but no officials were assaulted, no property was damaged, and the traditional effigies of the devil, the pope, and the pretender king were inscribed only with the innocuous slogan, "Liberty, Property, & no Commissioners." The Sons of Liberty made a very moderate show of force, but their show was punctuated by the perfect regulation of their men.

While Adams worked at the town meeting and in the streets to build confidence in his plan of resistance, he also labored in the House. Not long after his election, Adams proposed that the province pay to build a gallery onto the House chamber. Such a gallery, Adams suggested, would enable the people to watch over House proceedings and to keep informed on matters of colonial politics. Although there was little they could do to prevent this plan to edify Boston's voters, Tory officials easily saw through Adams's thinly veiled scheme. They cringed at the prospect of a gallery crammed full with every ranting Son of Liberty that Adams could muster. Political life, the Tories came to realize, would not be easy with Adams in the House.

Much of Adams's political strength derived from his new position as House clerk. He alone exercised the authority to keep notes on House debates, make official entries into the House journal, and safeguard that assembly's important documents and papers. In the winter of 1768, Adams worked the powers of his clerkship to the advantage of the popular party. On January 22, Adams made a motion for the House to publish a circular letter to the various colonies. Written collaboratively by Otis and Adams, the circular letter argued that Parliament had no power to tax the colonies for the purpose of raising revenue, and that the Townshend Duties therefore represented an unlawful infringement upon colonial rights.

To Adams's disappointment, the majority of the House stood in opposition to the motion. Tories feared that Adams's purpose was to prime the colonies for the convention of another congress, more radical than the assembly that met to debate the Stamp Act. Moderate Whigs, most of whom hailed from the Massachusetts countryside where the effects of the Townshend Acts were yet to be felt, refused to join Adams and Otis in their fight. The House voted overwhelmingly to defeat the motion.

But the House could not defeat Adams. He predicted that as winter dragged on, the ranks of conservative representatives from western Massachusetts would slowly thin out. Some rural delegates would leave to prepare for the planting season as soon as the ground began to thaw. Others, weary of the extended legislative session, would simply succumb to homesickness and return to their wives and families. Less than a month later, Adams's predictions had come true; most of the delegates had gone home, and the few who remained consisted primarily of radical Whigs who lived in Boston and its neighboring towns. On February 11, Adams once again moved that the House publish his circular letter. With little opposition, the motion passed. To conceal his shrewd machinations, Adams even ordered that all references to the prior, unsuccessful debate be removed from the House record.

Adams's campaign against the Townshend Act now began to heat up. Flush with the success of his circular letter, Adams scored another victory in March by persuading the House to approve his plan for nonimportation. Not long thereafter, Boston merchants agreed not to import a variety of goods until the duties had been repealed. Adams also set out to convince the people of New England that a grand conspiracy was afoot to rob the colonists of their liberties. He had railed for some time now—to anyone who would listen—against the royal customs officials. Their design, he argued, was to fill the colonies with informers until not a soul could be trusted.

Writing in the local papers as "A Puritan," Adams also spread rumors that the Archbishop of Canterbury intended to establish an American diocese, complete with its own bishop. Though there was little evidence to support that claim, such rumors resonated with Adams's Congregational countrymen, who for more than a century had guarded their religious freedom against royal encroachment. Adams then laid down his pen and took his campaign to the streets. His henchmen began harassing customs officials, hanging two in effigy. About the same time, the Sons of Liberty gathered to commemorate the repeal of the Stamp Act, and once again the night's festivities threatened to erupt into full-scale riots.

Back in England, news of the Massachusetts circular letter infuriated the king's ministers. Though the letter was no more radical than the Virginia or Massachusetts resolves of 1765, Crown officials had grown impatient with the Americans' insolence. Badly embarrassed by the circular letter, Governor Bernard ordered the House to adjourn. From London, Secretary of State Lord Hillsborough instructed the royal governors to prevent their legislatures from endorsing the circular letter, even if that meant disbanding the assemblies. But Hillsborough's instructions arrived too late. By May several colonies had followed Massachusetts' lead, including New Hampshire, Connecticut, New Jersey, and Virginia. Such insubordination was more than the English ministers could bear, and in June 1768, Lord Hillsborough made a fateful decision. Having for months read Governor Bernard's complaints that he could no longer maintain order in Boston, Hillsborough ordered that royal troops be sent to the town.

For the customs officials stationed in Boston, His Majesty's troops could not arrive soon enough. Though they had not yet made any major confiscations in Boston, customs officials had been tormented by Adams's confederates for months. Trade regulations were widely violated, and instead of cooperation, New England merchants offered the customs officials nothing but scorn. So long as the Massachusetts militia answered to Adams and his men, there was little the customs officials could do to enforce the duties. However, on May 17, a British man-of-war sailed into Boston harbor. Outfitted with fifty large cannons, the H.M.S. *Romney* had been sent by Lord Hillsborough to protect the Board of

In June 1768, Lord Hillsborough ordered several regiments of British troops to be sent to Boston to preserve order. Each soldier who enlisted in the British army and was sent to Boston received a certificate like this one.

Customs until troops could arrive in Boston. Emboldened by the *Romney*'s looming presence, the Board determined that the time had come to teach the Boston merchants a lesson. They chose to make an example out of none other than John Hancock, the colony's most wealthy and eminent merchant—and a close ally of Samuel Adams.

On May 9, Hancock's sloop, *Liberty,* arrived in port with a hull full of cargo. At that time the ship had been loaded and unloaded in the presence of customs officials, and tax had been paid on several barrels of Madeira wine. Yet on June 10, more than a month later, customs inspector Thomas Kirk charged that dutiable goods had been smuggled aboard the *Liberty*. What's more, Kirk declared that Hancock's captain had kept him locked up for several hours while the cargo was unlawfully taken ashore. On the basis of Kirk's statement, his colleague Benjamin Hallowell determined to seize Hancock's ship. (Perhaps not coincidentally, Hallowell was the same customs official whose house had been ripped apart during the Stamp Act riots.) While Hallowell delivered confiscation papers to the *Liberty*'s captain, a number of British marines boarded the sloop and towed it alongside the *Romney.*

Meanwhile a large crowd of sailors, dockhands, and townspeople had gathered on Hancock's wharf. As it became apparent that the *Liberty* was being confiscated, the crowd grew incensed. Some threw rocks at the marines as they hastily rowed back to their man-of-war, but most turned their attention to Hallowell and his assistants. As the mob began to close in, Hallowell perceived his danger and decided to run the gauntlet. He was beaten, knocked to the ground, and kicked several times before he could escape. Another official was assaulted and still a third was dragged through the streets by his hair. Having run off Hallowell and his men, the crowd then turned its anger against the officials' property. Perhaps aware of the irony that glass was a dutiable good, the crowd hurled stones through the windowpanes of officials' homes. The mob then seized a small boat belonging to one of the officials, carried it through the streets of Boston, and burned it at the foot of the Liberty Tree. By nightfall Boston had witnessed its largest riot in almost two years. And Samuel Adams had the satisfaction of knowing that he hadn't even planned it.

Adams's satisfaction was short-lived, for just a few days after the Liberty riots, the rumor broke that troops were headed for Massachusetts. The initial reaction was one of shock. Neither Adams nor his fellow Bostonians could believe the rumor was true. Never in the history of the colony had royal regiments been quartered in Boston. Soldiers! Stationed in Boston! The very idea was unfathomable. It violated basic principles of the English constitution—in particular, the principle that standing armies posed a danger to liberty.

As the rumor came to be confirmed, shock gave way to bitter resentment. To the people of New England it became increasingly clear that their rights as Englishmen meant nothing to the royal ministry. If outwardly indignant, though, inwardly the colonists suffered from apprehension, and even fear. Who would protect the townspeople from the soldiers? The militia was certainly no match for well-armed, well-trained veteran troops. Against such a force Adams's Liberty Boys were no more menacing than schoolchildren. What would become of the Patriot movement?

Governor Bernard could not have chosen a worse moment to pick a fight with the House of Representatives. But he had no choice. Acting on direct orders from Lord Hillsborough, Bernard called the legislature into session on June 21, and demanded that the representatives rescind Adams's circular letter. Had he asked just a few days earlier Bernard might have gotten the answer he wanted. Many of the representatives felt that Adams had tricked them, and they would have been all too happy to rescind the letter that they had voted against in the first place. But with troops on the way, the House was in no mood to be pushed around by Bernard. After a few days of impassioned oratory, the House voted, by an overwhelming margin of 92 to 17, to reject the governor's request. The circular letter would stand. Infuriated by the legislators' defiance, Governor Bernard once again disbanded the House.

The House's bold recalcitrance buoyed Samuel Adams's spirits, and for a time he worked frantically to hold the opposition movement together. Not willing to let the people of New England forget their former mettle, Adams rallied the Sons of Liberty on August 14 to celebrate the anniversary of the Stamp Act Riot. He then organized a town meeting to determine how Bostonians might best prepare themselves for royal troops. The town's first tack was to gather up, clean, and repair the muskets that had been collecting dust in the cellar of Faneuil Hall. Such measures, Adams coyly explained, were necessary to protect the town from invasion by the *French*. The town then took a more momentous step. Certain that Governor Bernard would not again convene the House until the British regiments arrived, the town called for a convention of delegates chosen from throughout Massachusetts.

On September 22, 1768, delegates from 67 towns, most of whom were also members of the House, met in Faneuil Hall. For five days the delegates debated their course of action. Adams soon discovered, though, that most of Massachusetts was bent on conciliation. The prospect of facing British troops had broken the will of many moderate Whigs. Several towns refused to send delegates, and James Otis didn't bother to take his seat for the first few days of the convention. Even more radical delegates were forced to admit the futility of fighting a large corps of British soldiers. So, after making a few remonstrances and passing the now boilerplate resolutions declaring the colonists' exclusive right to tax themselves, the Massachusetts convention adjourned. Most of the delegates left town immediately. Within a few days Boston was swarming with British soldiers.

text continues on page 80

CITIZENS AND SOLDIERS

In the wake of the Stamp Act Riots and various assaults on royal customs officials, Secretary of State Lord Hillsborough ordered in the summer of 1768 that British troops be stationed in Boston. Like most Whigs of the period, Samuel Adams believed that a standing army threatened the liberties of ordinary citizens. Adams also recognized that the Sons of Liberty were no match for well-armed Redcoats. So long as the soldiers inhabited the town, the resistance movement was virtually powerless. As he had done on so many previous occasions, Adams picked up his pen. Writing as "Vindex" in the December 12, 1768, edition of the Boston Gazette, *Adams hoped to rouse the townspeople against the quartering of troops. As he predicts in this letter, the conflict between citizens and soldiers would eventually culminate in the Boston Massacre.*

To the Printers.

It is a very improbable supposition, that any people can long remain free, with a strong military power in the very heart of their country: Unless that military power is under the direction of the people, and even then it is dangerous... Even when there is a necessity of the military power, within the land, which by the way but rarely happens, a wise and prudent people will always have a watchful & a jealous eye over it; for the maxims and rules of the army, are essentially different from the genius of a free people, and the laws of a free government. Soldiers are used to obey the absolute commands of their superiors: It is death for them, in the field, to dispute their authority, or the rectitude of their orders; and sometimes they may be shot upon the spot without ceremony.... Thus being inured to that sort of government in the field and in the time of war, they are too apt to retain the same idea, when they happen to be in civil communities and in a time of peace....

It is dangerous to civil society, when the military conceives of it self as an independent body, detach'd from the rest of the society, and subject to no controul: And the danger is greatly increased and becomes alarming, when the society itself yields to such an ill grounded supposition: If this should be the case, how easy would it be for the soldiers, if they alone should have the sword in their hands, to use it wantonly, and even to the great annoyance and terror of the citizens, if not to their destruction... And how long can we imagine it would be, upon such a supposition, before the tragical scene would begin... [T]hat people, who are not always on their guard to make use of the remedy of the constitution, when there is one, to restrain all kinds of power, and especially the military, from growing exorbitant, must blame themselves for the mischief that may befall them in consequence of their inattention: Or if they do not reflect on their own folly, their posterity will surely curse them, for entailing upon them chains and slavery.

I am led to these reflections from the appearance of the present times; when one wou'd be apt to think, there was like to be a speedy change of the civil, for a military government in this province... Military power is by no means calculated to convince the understandings of men: It may in another part of the world, affright women and children, and perhaps some weak men out of their senses, but will never awe a sensible American tamely to surrender his liberty. . . .

This we all know, and every child in the street is taught to know it; that while a people retain a just sense of liberty, as blessed be God, this people yet do, the insolence of power will for ever be despised; and that in a city, in the midst of civil society, especially in a time of peace, soldiers of all ranks, like all other men, are to be protected, govern'd, restrain'ed, rewarded or punsh'd by the Law of the Land.

Vindex.

text continued from page 77

For Samuel Adams and the Sons of Liberty, the months that followed were marked with despondency. As Redcoats marched in bright relief against overcast skies and snow-packed streets, the very landscape became a reminder that the town was under siege. Bernard and Hutchinson gleefully raised their cups with British officers, and Tory newspapers were quick to report the demise of the popular party.

As his Tory enemies celebrated their victory, Samuel Adams struggled to carve out a new role for himself and the popular party. The General Court still sat idle, the town meeting was essentially helpless, and riots, protests, and marches were obviously out of the question. All that remained for Adams was his pen. Almost as if to keep himself warm during the cold winter, Adams wrote vigorously. He filled the Boston papers with essays espousing the rights of the colonists. Using the pen name "Vindex," Adams spoke out against taxation without representation, and as "Candidus" he railed against the customs officials who preyed on innocent merchants and ship owners. In each of his essays, Adams drew on the Lockean political theory of government and the social compact that he had mastered at Harvard.

Adams also endeavored to keep the nonimportation movement alive, despite the objections of some New England merchants. He was happy to learn that in May 1769 Parliament had repealed the Townshend Duties on all goods except tea. The primary reason for the repeal was that the cost of enforcement was prohibitively high, but Adams was quick to give credit to the colonists' boycott. By trumpeting the fall of the Townshend Duties, Adams managed to convince the merchants to recommit themselves to nonimportation of British goods.

Yet the repeal of the Townshend Duties offered little joy to a town that was still occupied by British troops. Public buildings were given over to quarter the troops. Moonlighting soldiers stole jobs away from local workers.

Townspeople accustomed to coming and going as they pleased now found themselves challenged by British sentries. Samuel Adams hated the occupation so much that he trained his dog, Queue, to bark at the sight of a Redcoat. Nor were the soldiers happy to be in Boston. The hardships of military service were exacerbated by life overseas. Food was poor, a comfortable bed was nowhere to be found, and the people of Boston were rude and ungrateful. With every encounter, the people grew more impertinent and the Redcoats less patient.

Throughout the summer of 1769, the levels of friction between the Boston citizenry and royal troops and custom officials continued to rise. By July, Governor Bernard decided he had had enough. For nine arduous years he had held office, and he had survived more riots than he could count. He would not now preside over a powder keg and wait for it to explode. On August 1, Bernard boarded a ship bound for England, and he made no promise to return. Two weeks later, when the Sons of Liberty gathered once again to commemorate the Stamp Act Riots, they had even more reason to celebrate.

Soon after Bernard's departure a rapid series of events demonstrated just how tense Boston had become. The first involved Bernard's old nemesis, James Otis, Samuel and John Adams had for some time observed that Otis had been behaving erratically. On several occasions, such as when Otis declined to sit at the Massachusetts convention, his loyalty to the popular cause had come into question. Some thought Otis was torn between his love for the English monarchy and his hatred of Thomas Hutchinson. Others thought Otis was simply mad. He was subject to violent mood swings, began to drink heavily, and would rant so furiously in conversation that no one else could speak.

On September 5, Otis turned his fury against John Robinson, a customs official whom he had long detested. Otis approached Robinson in the Boston Coffee House and challenged him to a fight. The two men scuffled, and several British officers stepped in to assist the customs official. At some point during the melee, Otis suffered a severe blow to the head, possibly from a large cane that Robinson was known to carry. Although Otis survived the fight, John Adams reported that his mental condition deteriorated rapidly. Otis had at one point been considered the most brilliant legal mind in all of New England, but from his clash with Robinson until his death in 1783, 14 years later, his sanity continued to fade.

One month after Robinson "assassinated" Otis, the people of Boston witnessed another assault, this one even more dramatic and bizarre than Otis's coffeehouse brawl. The second incident appears to have been orchestrated by the Sons of Liberty, for it arose out of a conflict involving nonimportation. For several months Adams had labored tirelessly to sustain the boycott of British goods in the face of significant opposition from Boston merchants. Many merchants subscribed to Adams's nonimportation agreements only because they feared the wrath of the Sons of Liberty. Hungry for profits, some of those subscribers secretly continued to sell the boycotted goods.

For John Mein, publisher of the Tory newspaper, the *Boston Chronicle,* the hypocrisy of these traders was newsworthy material. In October, Mein began to list the names of merchants who were surreptitiously dealing goods that they had promised to boycott. Whether or not John Hancock and his fellow merchants had illicitly imported goods, they were embarrassed and angered by the *Chronicle's,* public accusation. Samuel Adams was even more enraged. Mein's exposé threatened to rip apart the boycott that Adams had so carefully knitted together. Not a merchant in the colony would continue the boycott while other merchants pocketed hefty profits. Mein had to be taught a lesson.

On October 28, "a large crowd of those who call themselves gentlemen" found Mein at the Boston Exchange. According to Elizabeth Cuming, a local merchant who opposed the nonimportation campaign, members of the crowd armed themselves with canes and spades, and chased the publisher through the streets, crying, "Kill him! Kill Him!" Blows fell one after another and pistol shots rang out. Yet somehow amid the tumult, Mein managed to find shelter in a guardhouse. Slowly the din subsided, and as darkness set in, it appeared that the crowd would disperse. But not long after dark, a large mob, perhaps as many as a thousand men and boys, paraded through town, dragging behind them a man in a cart. The victim was covered in tar and feathers, and so that the townspeople "might see the doleful Condition he was in," the mob forced him to carry a large glass lantern.

Strangely enough, the man in the "modern jacket" of tar and feathers was not John Mein, who ultimately fled to England, but rather a cus-toms informer by the name of George Gailer. Whether the men who chased Mein became the mob that tarred Gailer is unclear. It may be that the Sons of Liberty made Gailer a scapegoat because Mein had escaped, or it may be that two sepa-rate mobs arose. But the choice of Mein and Gailer as targets of Patriot violence was significant. Neither was a British officer, and though Gailer had informed against New England merchants, he did not actually work for the Board of Customs. The Sons of Liberty seemed to have realized that the British troops, whose ranks had

Waving banners for liberty and signing resolves for the nonim-portation of goods from Britain, the colonial people in this cartoon show their great desire to become an indepen-dent country.

recently been diminished by the withdrawal of two out of four regiments, would not step in to prevent Bostonians from attacking ordinary folk.

For several months Adams and his allies continued to pick their fights selectively, but fight they did, primarily in support of nonimportation. As Mein's *Chronicle* had made clear, some merchants were violating the boycott. If the Sons could not find a means to enforce the nonimportation agreement, it might collapse altogether. The Sons decided to intimidate importers with the threat of tar and feathers, a means of public humiliation that the colonists had only recently popularized. First introduced in Virginia in 1766, tar and feathers soon spread throughout the Atlantic seaboard. The tar brush was primarily used to paint the backs of snitches, such as George Gailer. But the Boston Sons of Liberty discovered that the mere hint of tar and feathers was sufficient to make merchants comply with the boycott. Throughout the winter and spring of 1770, Adams's accomplices tarred the windows and doors of merchants' shops and homes. In Marlborough, a small town to the west of Boston, the Sons of Liberty even tarred a merchant's horse!

This campaign of fear kept most of Boston's merchants in line, but on one occasion it erupted into violence. On February 21, 1770, the Sons tarred the home of an importer named Theophilus Lillie. The next day the Sons again assembled in front of Lillie's home, this time intending to hang him in effigy. At that moment one of Lillie's neighbors, a notorious customs informer named Ebenezer Richardson, began to harangue the crowd for its mischief. The crowd chased Richardson back into his home, beat on his doors, and hurled rocks through his windows. Fearing for his life, Richardson armed himself with a pistol and fired into the crowd. To the onlookers' horror, Richardson's bullet struck and killed an 11-year-old boy named Christopher Seider. In response, the crowd burst into Richardson's home, dragged him back into the streets, and prepared to hang him. Only

In a Gore of Blood

On October 28, 1769, a Boston crowd attacked newspaper publisher John Mein, who had printed the names of merchants who were violating Samuel Adams's nonimportation agreement. Mein managed to escape. That same day a mob assaulted a reputed customs informer named George Gailer. From the house of a family friend, Bostonian Elizabeth Cuming witnessed the two attacks. Cuming had reason to be afraid, because she and her sister, Anne, were merchants known to be importing goods from England.

On Saturday I was sitting in Madame Kints's chamber where she has been confined this three weeks with rheumatism, when we was alarmed with a violent screaming: 'Kill him! Kill him!' I flew to the window & to my great surprise saw Mr. Mein at the head of a large crowd of those who call themselves gentlemen, but in reality they were not other than murderers, for their design was certainly on his life. Some was armed with canes. Captain Marshall stopped at Mr. Waldo's shop & furnished himself with a spade, which he gave two thrusts at Mien with. Upon which, Mien fired a pistol he had in his hand, loaded only with powder, and ran into the guardhouse. By this time it was dark, our house shut up & we alone trembling like cowards, when a large mob of . . . a thousand men & boys arranged themselves before our door, & on a cart a man was exhibited as we thought in a gore of blood. Poor Mein we was sure was the sufferer but we was happily mistaken. It was an informer whom they had caught the moment Mien found shelter, & instantly hoisted him on a cart, tarred him all over, then feathered him—all under our window—then carried him through the town, obliging him to carry the lantern in his hand & calling for all the inhabitants to put candles in their windows.

the intervention of William Molineux, one of Adams's chief lieutenants, saved the informer's life.

Seider's murder inflamed the people of Boston. For almost a year their lives had been disrupted by riots, brawls, tar and feathers, and now a shooting. Thomas Hutchinson, who had been promoted to acting governor in Bernard's absence, was powerless to bring the sporadic violence to an end. British troops, instead of securing public order, only served to irritate the populace even more. Innocent people began to fear for their safety. Boston, once envisioned by its Puritan founders as "a citty upon a hill," now resembled nothing so much as Pandemonium, the demon-infested hell of John Milton's *Paradise Lost*. Yet, as unnerving as Boston's turmoil had been, the worst still lay ahead. Indeed, the months of disorder that followed the *Liberty* riots served only as a prelude of things to come.

March 5, 1770 was a cold, wind-swept day in Boston. Less than two weeks had passed since young Christopher Seider's death, and bitterness could still be seen in the towns-people's faces. The British troops were also on edge. For six long months the soldiers had been quartered in Boston, and it seemed that the relentless winter might never end. As dusk fell, Colonel William Dalrymple, the British commander, might have counted his blessings: another day had passed in peace. But the night would not. According to later reports, a tall, mysterious stranger appeared in the streets shortly after dark. Wearing a white wig and cloaked in a blood-red cape, the stranger stopped young men and warned them that Redcoats were out searching for townspeople to slaughter.

Meanwhile, near town hall on King Street, a single sentry named Private Hugh White stood watch at the guardhouse. Cold and alone, White had little patience for the crowd of boys who had begun to taunt him. White's patience contin-ued to dwindle as the boys, perhaps goaded by the mysteri-ous stranger, hurled snowballs and dared the soldier to fight. Suddenly, the bell of the First Church pealed through the wintry night. Those within earshot sprang from their beds; the church bell signaled a fire! Pouring out into the streets, the townspeople discovered no fire, but rather saw Private White arguing with a group of boys. To White's alarm the townspeople crowded in. White found himself surrounded. He anxiously called for assistance and was joined by his superior officer, Captain Thomas Preston, and a handful of fellow soldiers from the 29th regiment.

King Street was now packed with Redcoats and citizens. Captain Preston struggled to preserve order, but the crowd was too volatile. The townspeople continued to shout epithets at the soldiers, and some began to hurl chunks of ice. The mob crammed forward, and as its leaders came face to face with the Redcoats, they began pushing and shoving. Tense as they were, the soldiers held back. They could not fire unless ordered to do so. Just at that instant a soldier lost his footing on the icy pavement and fell to the ground. His gun discharged. Perhaps thinking they were under attack, or perhaps out of panic, Preston's men opened fire on the crowd.

Moments later, four Bostonians lay dead on King Street. Another lay dying and many others wounded.

Paul Revere's engraving of the Boston Massacre was an adroit piece of Patriot propaganda. Widely reprinted throughout the colonies, the engraving portrays British soldiers firing on an unarmed crowd of men and women. One building in the background bears the suggestive sign "Butcher's Hall."

TO SAVE THE COUNTRY

Above the din of the crowd and the sharp, ear-piercing report of muskets, Captain Preston somehow managed to make his cease-fire order heard. For a few, fleeting moments, King Street was silent. The townspeople and the Redcoats stared in shock at the dead and wounded who lay around them. The people then turned their eyes back to the soldiers. Solemnity gave way to vengeance and the crowd, clamoring for justice, again began to close in on the regiment. But before the mob could attack, Governor Hutchinson arrived from his office, where he had heard the gunshots. To his credit, Hutchinson was able to bring order to the mayhem. He first appeased the mob by ordering the arrest of Captain Preston and his men, and by promising to conduct a full judicial inquiry. Hutchinson then advised Colonel Dalrymple to order his men to their barracks. Left to tend to their casualties, the Bostonians slowly dispersed.

Daybreak brought the painful realization that the violent massacre was not just a horrible nightmare. In the early morning townspeople began to congregate at Faneuil Hall; soon their ranks swelled to such proportions that the meeting had to be relocated to the Old South meeting house. Stepping up into the pulpit, Samuel Adams urged his fellow citizens to stand firm in defense of their liberties. Meanwhile, word that the Redcoats had fired on innocent, unarmed town folk spread throughout the Massachusetts countryside. Local militias began to rise, and messengers arrived carrying pledges of support for the Boston Patriots.

Indignant and emboldened, the people appointed a committee of 15 men to petition Governor Hutchinson for the withdrawal of troops from the town. With the likes of Molineux, Hancock, and Warren at his side, Samuel Adams marched to the Council chamber and demanded to be heard. There, before Dalrymple, Hutchinson, and several councilors, Adams insisted that nothing less than "a total and immediate removal of the troops" would satisfy the people. With steely determination, Adams looked Hutchinson in the eye. "It is at your peril," he proclaimed, "if you refuse."

Hutchinson squirmed in his seat. Flustered, he attempted to excuse himself. As governor, he demurred, he had no power over the troops. But Adams was steadfast, and Hutchinson recognized just how dire the situation was. After conferring with his councilors, Hutchinson convinced Dalrymple to withdraw his men to Castle William. His only condition was that Adams provide assurances that the troops would not be harassed as they left town. On March 10, five days after the massacre and just two days after funeral services were held for the victims, Dalrymple and his men marched from their barracks to the harbor. At their side, Adams's lieutenant William Molineux rode on horseback, a lone escort ensuring the safey of hundreds of troops.

In the aftermath of the massacre, Boston Whigs of course found many opportunities to rail against British tyranny. Paul Revere immortalized the slain with an engraving of the bloody massacre, and Adams filled the papers with exhortations against oppression at the hands of a standing army. There was also, however, a defensive element to the Whigs' propaganda. Some Tories had already begun to whisper that

Adams had orchestrated the clash to incite the townspeople. A few speculated that Adams himself was the red-cloaked instigator on the dock that night. Even more damaging than Tory rumors was the confession of Patrick Carr, an Irishman who was shot during the massacre but survived for a few days. As he lay dying Carr declared that the towns-people had provoked the attack and that the soldiers fired only in self-defense. If not refuted, such stories threatened to quell the people's fury and also to undermine Adams and the Boston Patriots.

Hutchinson delayed the trials until the fall, and in the meantime Captain Preston and his men sought about for defense attorneys that could save them from the gallows. Not surprisingly, most of the lawyers of Boston were reluctant to take the case. In the eyes of the townspeople, Preston's troops had committed a vile crime, and the lawyer who chose to defend these men risked ruining his own standing in the community. John Adams, however, strongly believed in every accused individual's right to defense counsel. Like the right to trial by jury, or the right to confront witnesses, the right to an attorney was an important cornerstone of the English judicial system. If no one volunteered to defend the soldiers, John's conscience would compel him to step forward.

Meanwhile, John's elder cousin, Samuel, recognized that the outcome of the soldiers' trial threatened to harm the Patriot resistance movement. On the one hand, the jury might acquit the soldiers and blame the massacre on the Liberty Boys who had provoked His Majesty's troops. On the other, the jury might convict the soldiers too quickly or impose severe penalties, causing the people of England and America to think the trial was a sham and that Boston was a vengeful, unjust town. If, however, the attorneys who rep-resented the soldiers were friendly to the Patriot cause, they might be able to defend their clients without casting the people of Boston or the Sons of Liberty in a negative light. So, for motives very different from John's, Samuel urged his

SAMUEL ADAMS

cousin to take the case. On Samuel's advice, John Adams and Josiah Quincy agreed to represent Preston and his men in spite of public opinion.

In Adams and Quincy, the soldiers benefited from two of the colony's best legal minds. The duo did a masterly job of defending the troops. Their first coup was to empanel a jury composed mostly of non-Bostonians; this jury's verdict would emanate from reason, rather than revenge. Adams and Quincy also managed to keep their cross-examination limited. Little was heard about the red-cloaked stranger or the mischievous rumors he spread about blood-thirsty Redcoats. Finally, Adams and Quincy convinced the jury that Preston's men had fired only to protect themselves from an incendiary mob of slaves, saucy boys, and sailors. Neither the soldiers nor the *good people* of Boston could be blamed for such an unfortunate incident. This strategy produced the desired effect. The jury acquitted Captain Preston and convicted only two soldiers of the reduced charge of manslaughter.

Though the official, courtroom story told of the soldiers' innocence, the popular, street-gossip story told of their guilt. Again writing as Vindex, Samuel Adams used local newspapers to sway public opinion in favor of the resistance movement. Recounting the Redcoats' many atrocities, he lambasted the jury for setting the prisoners free, and swore that had a single patriot sat on the panel, the soldiers would have been brought to justice. Yet Adams protected the reputation of the defense attorneys by praising John Adams and Josiah Quincy for admirably performing an undesirable task. Their defense work, Vindex suggested, protected the rights of the soldiers, even though those soldiers had violated the rights of English citizens. If Samuel Adams's account were to be believed, the people of Boston stood firmly on the moral high ground.

For a time, Adams managed to keep the New England populace agitated over the massacre. But after the trials, as the legal dust began to settle, Adams saw that support for the popular cause had begun to wane once again. His Majesty's troops, long the bugbear of all liberty-loving New Englanders, were now encamped harmlessly behind the walls of Castle William, and many Bostonians prayed that the time was finally ripe for peace. Parliament had seen fit to repeal the Townshend Duties on every import but tea, and royal duties were as low as they had been in decades. News also arrived from England that King George III had officially promoted Thomas Hutchinson to replace Bernard as governor. Though Hutchinson had his enemies, Samuel Adams chief among them, many Massachusetts citizens were delighted that the king had so generously appointed a native-born Bostonian to serve as governor. To Adams's disgust, the people of New England felt, for the moment at least, that they had little cause to resent the imperial administration.

Adams might also have bristled to think that he was partly responsible for the decline of the Boston Whigs. Not long before the massacre, Boston voters ousted James Otis, whose ranting and raving had grown too disruptive to ignore, from the House of Representatives. For years, Otis, a moderate, had kept Adams's radicalism in check. As Otis slowly lost his sway over the Whig party, the popular cause continued to move in Adams's direction. But many New Englanders felt Adams pushed too far. His refusal to compromise on nonimportation and his consistent opposition to Parliament made a poor impression on more moderate citizens. And notwithstanding Adams's efforts at restraint, some colonists agreed with those Tories who blamed the Sons of Liberty for Boston's public disturbances. Adams's campaign against importing merchants seemed particularly brutal given how little the boycotts ultimately accomplished. The people were exceedingly weary of violence, and increasingly distrustful of radicalism.

The first indication that the Whig movement was slipping came from the collapse of the nonimportation agreement. Samuel Adams was uniquely enamored of his nonimportation scheme. He loathed the colonists' dependency on British goods, and he yearned for the day when Americans would clothe themselves in American wool and furnish their homes with American goods.

Few colonists shared Adams's vision. The very idea of a self-sufficient economy struck most colonists as preposterous; American industry was far too young and its labor far too scarce. Indifferent as they were to economic independence, many shopkeepers and merchants called for an end to non-importation as soon as the Townshend Duties were repealed. New York and Philadelphia argued against the boycotts, and the Massachusetts towns outside of Boston were also eager to import. In August 1770, Samuel Adams sent William Molineux to convince merchants in Salem to stay the non-importation course. So firm was Salem opposition that Molineux was chased out of town by a mob threatening to tar and feather *him*. In October, Adams had no choice but to remain silent as Boston merchants voted to end the boycott.

Even in the House of Representatives, where he had risen through the ranks just a few years before, Samuel Adams felt his influence decline. In January 1770, Lord Hillsborough instructed Hutchinson to move the House from Boston to Cambridge. On the western banks of the Charles, where Adams was forced to labor without the benefit of his Liberty Boys to pack the gallery or the *Gazette* to publish his diatribes, Tories found their political lives much improved. Adams, of course, protested loudly against the king's right to relocate the people's assembly, and he demanded that the governor return the House to Boston. Hutchinson merely scoffed at Adams's pretense. Who was this coarse provincial to say just what the king could or could not do?

Compounding Adams's troubles was the loss of two key members of the Whig party. Weary from the massacre trial, John Adams returned to his home in Braintree, 15 miles south of Boston. The departure of Samuel's talented kinsman deprived the Boston resistance movement of one of its best minds and most forceful pens. Even more devastating, how-ever, was the faithlessness of John Hancock, the party's chief financial backer.

For years now Hancock had been losing money on Adams, and his forays into politics had caused him to neglect his business. By all accounts, Hancock was also extraordinarily vain. Mindful of both his popularity and success, he did not want to sink aboard Adams's ship. He fired John Adams as his attorney, and he allowed his relations with Samuel to sour. Governor Hutchinson, meanwhile, took note of this growing rift and began to court the wealthy young merchant. The governor offered Hancock a military appointment as colonel of cadets, which Hancock eagerly accepted, and he insinuated that if Hancock would only repent his Whiggish ways, he might also find a seat on the governor's council.

Adams began to grow despondent. He had witnessed slumps before but nothing so devastating as this. He was now almost 50 years old, and the vicissitudes of political life had begun to take their toll on the old Patriot. His hair had turned gray and his colleagues observed that Adams had developed a palsy; his hands trembled as he wrote. Adams was never one to pay much attention to his appearance. He cared little whether his suits were worn or his cap a little tattered. But for those around him, Adams's outward bearing seemed to reflect his inward condition. Some even began to wonder whether Adams's political career might be nearing an end. Certainly his popularity continued to wane. Tories harangued Adams about his failure to collect taxes, claiming that he had embezzled the funds to finance his Sons of Liberty. So much did Adams's career falter that in 1771 he lost an election for the minor post of Registrar of Deeds for Suffolk County; a Tory beat him by a margin of 2 to 1.

There was, however, a bright spot in Adams's political career, and it could be found, ironically enough, in his rela-tions with the towns outside of Boston and with the other colonies. In an effort to build support for nonimportation,

Adams had for some time been writing letters to like-minded Whigs throughout New England. In the fall of 1772, he decided to formalize these ties by reorganizing the inter-colonial committees of correspondence.

Such committees first came into existence during the Stamp Act crisis, and they formed the loose network of communication that linked the various Patriot organizations throughout the colonies. In their letters, committee mem-bers shared grievances against royal tyranny and plotted strategies of resistance. Indeed, it was these organizations that made collaborative action possible. Adams hoped that by reviving these committees he might also breath life into his flagging popular party. On November 2, 1772, the Boston town meeting voted in favor of Adams's motion to appoint a committee of correspondence. Other Massachusetts towns followed suit, and the following spring, the Virginia House of Burgesses called for correspondence as well.

Meanwhile, in local politics, Adams still struggled to reclaim his former stature. His efforts were nearly thwarted in the spring of 1772, when John Hancock and Thomas Cushing managed to accomplish what Adams could not: they convinced Hutchinson to move the House of Repre-sentatives back to Boston. Unlike stubborn Samuel Adams, Hancock and Cushing were willing to concede the king's right to relocate the assembly. This gracious concession was enough for Governor Hutchinson, who was happy to drive a wedge between Adams and his former allies. Soon thereafter the House nominated Hancock to serve on Hutchinson's council, and Hutchinson, convinced that Hancock could be manipulated, approved of the nomination.

For a time it appeared that Hancock might assume control of the popular party and push it in a more conservative direction. Adams was far too obstinate to seek a reconciliation with his old ally, and Hancock far too proud. But several Boston Whigs recognized the danger of a split in their party, and they began working to bring the estranged leaders back together. Mutual friends reminded Adams that the cause could not easily make do without Hancock's financial support. They reminded Hancock that his popularity derived from the people rather than from a few well-to-do Tories. The gentlemen were thus reunited, and to Hutchinson's dismay, Hancock refused to sit on his council. Hancock celebrated his renewed alliance with Adams by commissioning the respected New England artist John Singleton Copley to paint Adams's portrait. Hancock hung the portrait in his drawing room, next to a portrait of himself that Copley had painted years before, as a reminder of their friendship. But it would not be the last time that Adams and he would fall out of grace with one another.

Adams had survived the discord within his own party, but he could not avoid the fact that New Englanders were in a complacent mood. He began to grope for issues around which the people might rally; any instance of despotism would suffice. For a time Adams made much of the fact that the king had assumed responsibility for Hutchinson's salary. Paying the governor had been a right of Massachusetts citizens for over a century, even though the position was appointed by the Crown. The ability to cut a governor's salary or to withhold it altogether provided a powerful check on that executive's power. Now that salaries were to be paid out of the royal treasury, the governor would be accountable only to the Crown.

Adams was quick to draw attention to this latest form of tyranny, and when in 1772 rumor reached Boston that the

text continues on page 100

This portrait by John Singleton Copley depicts John Hancock as a wealthy merchant: fashionably attired, he sits with his ledger book, quill in hand. Hancock commissioned Copley to paint a portrait of Samuel Adams to hang alongside his own when the two Patriots were reunited after a brief falling out.

THE RIGHTS OF THE COLONISTS

In the fall of 1772, the Massachusetts Whig party was on the decline. In order to revive the popular movement, Adams organized committees of correspondence through-out the colonies. Through these committees Adams circulated a declaration entitled, "The Rights of the Colonists." Though written four years before the Declaration of Independence, this document expressed many of the beliefs that would later provide the justification for revolution. The following selections are taken from Section I, Natural Rights of the Colonists as Men, and Section III, The Rights of the Colonists as Subjects.

Among the natural rights of the Colonists are these: First, a right to life; Secondly, to liberty; Thirdly, to property; together with the right to support and defend them in the best manner they can.

All men have a right to remain in a state of nature as long as they please; and in case of intolerable oppression, civil or religious, to leave the society they belong to, and enter into another....

The natural liberty of man is to be free from any superior power on earth, and not to be under the will or legislative authority of man, but only to have the law of nature for his rule....

If men, through fear, fraud, or mistake, should in terms renounce or give up any essential natural right, the eternal law of reason and the grand end of society would absolutely vacate such renunciation. The right to freedom being the gift of God Almighty, it is not in the power of man to alienate this gift and voluntarily become a slave....

A commonwealth or state is a body politic, or civil society of men, united together to promote their mutual safety and prosperity by means of their union.

The absolute rights of Englishmen, and all freemen, in or out of civil society, are principally personal security, personal liberty, and private property....

Now what liberty can there be where property is taken away without consent? Can it be said with any color of truth and justice, that this continent of three thousand miles in length, and of a breadth as yet unexplored, in which, however, it is supposed there are five millions of people, has the least voice, vote, or influence in the British Parliament? Have they all together any more weight or power to return a single member to that House of Commons who have not inadvertently, but deliberately, assumed a power to dispose of their lives, liberties, and properties, than to choose an Emperor of China?... The inhabitants of this country, in all probability, in a few years, will be more numerous than those of Great Britain and Ireland together; yet it is absurdly expected by the promoters of the present measures that these, with their posterity to all generations, should be easy, while their property shall be disposed of by a House of Commons at three thousand miles' distance from them, and who cannot be supposed to have the least care or concern for their real interest; who have not only no natural care for their interest, but must be in effect bribed against it, as every burden they lay on the Colonists is so much saved or gained to themselves.... The Colonists have been branded with the odious names of traitors and rebels only for complaining of their grievances. How long such treatment will or ought to be borne, is submitted.

text continued from page 97

ministry also intended to place colonial judges on the king's payroll, Adams picked up his pen once again. Calling himself "Valerius Poplicola," after one of the first consuls of the Roman Republic, Adams opined that royal pensioners felt no loyalty to the people. Where they went, abuse of power was sure to follow. With impassioned rhetoric Adams asked of his fellow citizens, "Is it not High Time for the People of this Country explicitly to declare, whether they will be Freemen or Slaves?"

Adams worried about the docility that surrounded him. The people of New England, he believed, had begun to take their rights for granted, and were therefore vulnerable to imperial oppression. Adams felt that his patriotic duty required him to keep the colonists vigilant. As he explained, "The *true patriot*...will, as far as he is able, keep the attention of his fellow citizens awake to their grievances; and not suffer them to be at rest, till the causes of their just complaints are removed." In keeping with this spirit, in the fall of 1772 Adams penned an extensive document entitled "The Rights of the Colonists." This manifesto defined in detail the rights of colonists as men, as Christians, and as subjects of the English Crown. Steeped in the natural-rights ideology of John Locke, Adams's "Rights" anticipated the Declaration of Independence by four years. "Among the natural rights of the Colonists," Adams proclaimed, "are these: First, a right to life; Secondly, to liberty; Thirdly, to property."

Adams also hinted at the possibility of revolution: "All men have a right to remain in a state of nature as long as they please; and in case of intolerable oppression, civil or religious, to leave the society they belong to, and enter into another." Ardent as Adams's declarations were, they had not been written in response to any particular act of oppression, but rather as part of Adams's ongoing efforts to stoke the fire of resistance. In keeping with his mission as a "true patriot," Adams appended to his "Rights" a list of infringements and violations committed by the royal government. He then circulated these declarations among the committees of correspondence.

Unfortunately for Adams, most Massachusetts colonists did not share his concerns about British despotism. The Crown's assumption of gubernatorial and judicial salaries was indeed irksome, but it was not the sort of issue that would send the otherwise satisfied citizens up in arms. Nor did most colonists yet believe that Adams's question "Freemen or Slaves?" properly framed the discussion about imperial politics. So long as taxes were low and troops out of sight, the majority of New Englanders favored peace with the mother country. Though he took some satisfaction from the ever-expanding network of committees of correspondence, Adams was forced to bide his time. But in the early months of 1773, he began to wonder just what it would take to wake his neighbors from their political slumber.

In the spring, Adams found his answer. It came in the form of a packet of documents that Benjamin Franklin forwarded from England. At the time, Franklin was serving abroad as a colonial agent and as the postmaster general for the colonies. Through his connections in London, Franklin managed to gain possession of a series of letters written by Adams's long-time nemesis, Thomas Hutchinson. Hutchinson had written the letters to a former member of Parliament named Thomas Whately, and they were not, on the whole, particularly inflammatory.

But Franklin recognized that the letters did contain some language that the people of New England might find offensive. Franklin had been hoping for an opportunity to demonstrate his loyalty to the American cause, and so he shipped the letters to the Boston Whig, Thomas Cushing, who immediately turned them over to Samuel Adams. Franklin did not, however, want Hutchinson's blood on his hands, and he specifically instructed the Boston Whigs neither to copy the letters nor to circulate them among more than a few trusted allies.

Unfortunately for Franklin, Adams's glee could not contain itself. Hutchinson's plural office holding and his aristocratic bearing represented for Adams all of the evils of the British Empire. Moreover, Hutchinson had feuded with the Adams family for 30 years. He had lobbied against the land bank, upheld the writs of assistance, and supported the Stamp Act, all in the service of a corrupt royal government. His triumphant appointment as governor did nothing to stem his ambition. In his second year of office Hutchinson nearly divided the ranks of the popular party by courting John Hancock.

More recently, Hutchinson had vetoed John Adams's nomination to his council, and in a pointed rebuttal to Samuel's "Rights of the Colonists," Hutchinson had argued extensively in favor of the supremacy of Parliament. For Adams there was no greater enemy of colonial liberty than the governor. Now Adams held in his hands the means not only to destroy his foe, but also to whip the popular movement into a radical frenzy. Never had two birds sat so prettily for one stone.

For several weeks, Boston Whigs spread rumors that secret information revealing a grand conspiracy to suppress the rights of American colonists had been obtained. On June 2, 1773, Adams announced before the House of Representatives that he now held conclusive evidence that implicated several New Englanders in this conspiracy, including one of high rank. He dramatically ordered that all spectators be expelled from the gallery and that the doors be barred. He then read Hutchinson's letters to a suspense-filled House. But Adams did not stop there. He also concocted a scheme to circumvent Franklin's instructions.

Shortly after Adams's address, John Hancock took the floor and declared that some anonymous person on the Common had presented him with a manuscript copy of Hutchinson's letters. That copy, of course, could have come only from the pen of Samuel Adams. Yet under the pretense that the letters were already circulating among the general public, Whig leaders agreed that Hancock's copy could now be published. In this way, Adams and the Whigs were able to expose Hutchinson and still remain in strict compliance with the letter, if not the spirit, of Franklin's order. (In London, Franklin was publicly humiliated for his role in the affair, and was fired as postmaster general.)

Within a fortnight, Hutchinson's letters had been printed as a pamphlet for distribution throughout New England. The Boston Committee of Correspondence saw to it that the letters were also forwarded throughout the colonies. Meanwhile, Adams arranged for the more reprehensible letters to be published in the *Gazette*.

Sensible that the subtleties of Hutchinson's letters might be lost on the average reader, Adams took great liberties with the governor's text. He rearranged sentences, minced paragraphs, and quoted out of context, much to Hutchinson's disadvantage. By the time Adams was through with the letters, Hutchinson appeared blameworthy for every public malady from the Stamp Act to the Boston Massacre. Most damning of all was Hutchinson's conclusion that the vast distance between the colonies and the mother country, and the attendant difficulties of colonial governance, necessitated "an abridgement of what are called English liberties." Here was proof that Hutchinson had, in fact, proposed that the colonists' rights be restricted.

The governor was deeply wounded. He knew that the "great incendiary," as he now referred to Adams, could go to extremes. Hutchinson was, after all, the same man whose home had been ransacked by the Boston mob. But now Hutchinson felt that Adams had gone too far. Comparing his Whig enemy to a modern-day Machiavelli, Hutchinson wrote that, for Adams, the public good was "above all other considerations." By publishing his private letters, Adams had transgressed the boundaries of honor and dispensed with "every rule of morality."

Throughout this episode Adams adhered to a maxim that became the cornerstone of his career and that, if not entirely Machiavellian, at least made for merciless political strategy: "Put your adversary in the wrong, and keep him there." Certainly in the eyes of the people of Massachusetts, Hutchinson was in the wrong. Public outcry was enormous; even Hutchinson's friends in the Tory-dominated countryside began to turn their backs on the governor. The House of Representatives resolved that a plan had been formed

> by a set of men, born and educated among us, to raise their own fortunes, and advance themselves to posts of honor and profit, not only to the destruction of the charter and constitution of this province, but at the expense of the rights and liberties of the American colonies.

The House also voted overwhelmingly to petition King George for Hutchinson's removal from office. Naturally, Samuel Adams wrote the draft of that petition.

Adams could not have chosen a more propitious moment to discredit the governor. At the height of the Hutchinson scandal, word arrived from England that Parliament had passed a new piece of legislation known as the Tea Act. Tea was the only commodity for which the Townshend Acts had not been repealed; the colonists still paid a three-pence tax for every pound of English tea. Like most British subjects, however, Americans cherished their tea. Wealthier colonists spent lavish sums on teacups, teaspoons, teapots, tea trays, and tea tables. Men and women of fashion even entertained in tea rooms. So much was tea in vogue that James Otis, in a lucid moment, proclaimed that the colonists might "part with all their liberties, and religion too, rather than renounce it." But instead of parting with their liberties, most colonists simply avoided the Townshend duty by smuggling Dutch tea. American merchants had for several years raked in huge profits on this illicit trade.

This British cartoon satirized the ladies of Edenton, North Carolina, for signing a resolution not to consume tea from England. Engaging in politics, the cartoon suggests, had corrupted American women, who sipped punch and flirted with men while eschewing their domestic duties.

In England, meanwhile, tea supplies began to back up. Warehouses overflowed with stores of tea that could not be sold, and the East India Company, London's largest tea distributor, found itself on the brink of bankruptcy. In order to save the company, the Prime Minister of England, Lord Frederick North, proposed the Tea Act. This law granted the East India Company the right to trade directly with the colonists, rather than through London merchants. By eliminating these middlemen, the company was able to cut the cost of tea dramatically. Even though the three-pence duty was not repealed, the East India Company could now offer prices much lower than those that Americans currently paid for smuggled Dutch tea.

In fact, American tea prices would fall to less than half of what was paid back in England. Lord North congratulated himself for devising such a generous system.

Yet in the eyes of American colonists, the Tea Act was anything but generous. Even though the price of tea would drop, part of that price would include the three-pence duty. Samuel Adams and other Whig leaders were loath to pay the duty because such a payment would implicitly acknowledge Parliament's authority to levy taxes on the colonists. The Tea Act also threatened to put a pinch on colonial trade. American merchants recognized that the new legislation would bring a halt to their lucrative smuggling profits. Worse than this, the East India Company could now pick and choose the American merchants with whom it would trade. In effect, the East India Company now enjoyed a monopoly over the distribution of tea, and it was obvious that most colonial merchants would be cut out of the loop.

The Tea Act played brilliantly into Samuel Adams's hands. Having discredited Governor Hutchinson and once again bolstered support for the popular party, Adams was well situated to foment resistance to the new law. However, in a rare reversal of roles, the earliest and most vehement opposition to the Tea Act came neither from Massachusetts nor Virginia, but rather from Pennsylvania and New York. In those erstwhile placid colonies, merchants had smuggled enormous amounts of tea from the Dutch, and these merchants were significantly more organized than those in other colonies.

In Philadelphia, the so-called Committee for Tarring and Feathering threatened to turn their tar brushes against any tea consignee who dared distribute the English tea. The Committee also admonished the pilots of the Delaware River not to "make a Goose" of themselves—that is, not to earn a coat of tar and feathers—by navigating tea-laden ships into port. Such threats were more than enough to convince the tea distributors to forego their monopoly rights. In Boston, though, the tea consignees put up more of a fight. These merchants included Thomas and Elisha Hutchinson, the sons of the governor who was still reeling from the blow Adams had dealt only months before. Now more than ever before, Hutchinson intended to stand firm in the face of Adams and the Sons of Liberty.

Hutchinson got his first opportunity on November 2, at the yawning hour of 2 A.M. Then, while most Bostonians slept fast in their beds, Hutchinson was rudely awakened by a loud knock on his door. Adams's Liberty Boys were calling, and they demanded that Hutchinson meet the public at the Liberty Tree that day at noon. Their purpose of course was to force Hutchinson to resign as tea consignee, just as Andrew Oliver had resigned as Stamp Act Commissioner eight years before. But Hutchinson was steadfast. Neither he nor any other of the consignees appeared at the Liberty Tree, despite repeated threats by the Sons of Liberty. On November 17, a large crowd gathered on Hutchinson's lawn, again reminiscent of the mob that had destroyed his home during the Stamp Act riots. Yet the governor remained defiant.

Ten days later, the *Dartmouth,* a cargo ship filled with East India tea, sailed into Boston Harbor and docked at Griffin's Wharf. Samuel Adams feared that the tea might secretly be unloaded and sold throughout New England. Several weeks earlier at a town meeting presided over by John Hancock, the people of Boston agreed not to import the tea. But Adams was not willing to take any chances, and so his committee of correspondence appointed several men to stand watch over the *Dartmouth.*

Adams and his fellow Whigs now found themselves in a bit of a quandary. Unwilling to pay the duty, they hoped the captain would simply sail his ship back to England. But as Hutchinson was quick to observe, British law prohibited the *Dartmouth* from returning home unless duties had been paid on all of her freight, even if that freight had never been unloaded. So, as Boston Whigs fretfully observed, the tea could neither be unloaded nor returned; one way or the other, taxes would have to be paid. To complicate matters, British law further required that all duties be paid within twenty days after a ship reached port. The *Dartmouth*'s duties therefore came due on December 17. If the taxes were not tendered by then, Hutchinson would order the troops stationed at Castle William to unload the ship, customs officials would seize its cargo, the tea would be sold, and the duty paid.

Something had to be done. As the Boston Whigs were painfully aware, the Sons of Liberty in Pennsylvania and New York had begun to question the courage of their New England brethren. On November 29 and again on December 14, the town requested that Governor Hutchinson return the tea. The governor smugly responded that he would be happy to do so, if only the people would suffer the duties to be paid. At last, Hutchinson thought, he had beaten Samuel Adams. But once again he underestimated his arch rival.

Early in the day of December 16, as the clock ticked down on the deadline for payment of the duties, Samuel Adams convened a town meeting. A throng of citizens attended, including many from the countryside, where Adams's committees of correspondence had shored up support for the resistance movement. The people quickly overflowed Faneuil Hall; Adams estimated that more than 5,000 New Englanders were present. So, as in years past, the meeting adjourned to the Old South Church. Those in attendance voted that the captain be sent once again to ask Governor Hutchinson whether he might be permitted to sail for England. The governor had retired to his home in Milton, and it took the captain several hours to return. In the meantime, Boston Whigs kept the audience in a fever with speech after speech of fiery rhetoric. Just as darkness fell, Captain Rotch stepped back through the doors of the Old South. The governor had refused his request.

Samuel Adams rose before the crowd, his heart racing in expectation of what was to come. Looking out at the faces of his townspeople, he might even have trembled to think of the consequences of what he was about to do. But if Adams had second thoughts, he did not let them stop him. In a commanding voice, Adams proclaimed, "This meeting can do nothing more to save the country!" Adams's words provoked a chorus of fierce war cries, and upon this signal several hundred Sons of Liberty marched to Griffin's Wharf. Thinly disguised as Narragansett Indians, this corps of Patriots boarded the *Dartmouth* and several sister ships. The men then proceeded to dump the tea. Working methodically and in complete silence, the Liberty Boys emptied 342 chests into Boston Harbor. In four hours' time they had completed their task, and the "Tea Party"—as it came to be known decades later—was over.

On December 16, Adams's Liberty Boys, disguised as Narragansett Indians, dumped 342 chests of tea into Boston Harbor. Throngs of Bostonians watched in silence from nearby wharves.

Americans throwing the Cargoes of the Tea Ships into the River, at Bofton

7

THE COERCIVE ACTS AND THE CONTINENTAL CONGRESS

Samuel Adams celebrated New Year's Eve, 1773, by writing a letter to his friend and fellow radical, Arthur Lee of Virginia. Two weeks had passed since the "Mohawks," as Adams's Liberty Boys had come to be known, hurled the tea into the harbor, but Adams was still just as rhapsodic as he had been that very night. "You cannot imagine," he exclaimed, "the height of joy that sparkles in the eyes and animates the countenances as well as the hearts of all we meet."

Except of course for "the disappointed, disconcerted Hutchinson and his tools," the citizens of Boston had much cause for jubilation. The Tea Party was a bold stroke in defense of the colonists' liberties, far more defiant than the Stamp Act protests. And yet, the destruction of the tea had been carried out with a degree of orderliness and dignity. No houses had been ransacked, and no persons had been threatened or harmed. The townspeople, rather, had made every possible effort to ship the tea back to England, and only when those efforts failed did they resort to dumping it into the bay. In the midst of the raid, the Patriots had shown their respect for law and property by replacing the locks they had broken off the hold of the ships. Even

Boston's more moderate Whigs could embrace such a restrained act of resistance. Samuel's cousin, John Adams, confessed that he was charmed by the "Sublimity" of the Tea Party, and he spoke for many New Englanders when he declared it to be "the grandest Event which has ever yet happened Since the Controversy with Britain opened!"

News of the grand event spread quickly through the colonies. Within a few days the Sons of Liberty in Philadelphia and New York were singing the praises of the intrepid New Englanders, and Virginia and South Carolina soon joined the chorus. Nowhere, though, was the excitement as great as it was in Massachusetts. Boston had once again moved to the fore in the fight against ministerial oppression, and its townspeople felt jubilant. Indeed, the dumping of the tea seemed to electrify the town, charging the winter air with revolutionary energy.

As had been the case during the Stamp Act, though, the people of Boston, once agitated, could not be easily contained, and on January 25, 1774, they formed a violent mob in King Street. The incident arose early in the afternoon, when a small boy pushed a sled across the path of Captain John Malcom, a much-despised customs official who had been tarred and feathered in New Hampshire just a couple of months before. Captain Malcom was "a hottempered man and he began cursing and threatening the boy with his heavy cane. At that moment a young shoemaker named George Robert Twelves Hewes intervened, and urged the captain not to strike the child. Infuriated that this "boy" should dare to tell a gentleman his business, Captain Malcom insulted Hewes, calling him a vagabond. Hewes replied that he, at least, had never been tarred and feathered. This fresh affront incensed the customs officer. As a gentleman of distinction, Malcom felt obliged to defend his honor against the insults of a lowly tradesman. He lifted his cane and, with a furious blow, struck the young shoemaker across the head.

Word of the assault quickly spread, and the people of Boston felt less sympathy for Malcom's wounded honor than for Hewes's wounded head. That evening, after Hewes had received medical treatment and sworn out a warrant for Malcom's arrest, a large crowd gathered at the captain's home and dragged him into the street. Sensing the danger, several gentlemen attempted to appease the throng, promising that Malcom would be brought to justice in a court of law. For years Boston crowds had acted with restraint, rallying only at the behest of the Sons of Liberty. But the Tea Party had emboldened the townspeople, and they were now determined to act of their own volition.

Heedless of the gentlemen's pleas, the mob stripped Captain Malcom, beat him, and subjected him to his second coat of tar and feathers. As Hewes later remembered, Malcom was paraded on a sled to the Liberty Tree, to the gallows on Boston Neck, to Butcher's Hall, to Charlestown Ferry, then to Copp's Hill. At every stop he was flogged. The crowd then found some tea and forced Malcom to drink the loathsome, boycotted beverage until he was ill. After several hours of this torture, the mob finally deposited Malcom, bloodied, bruised, and frostbitten, on his doorstep.

Samuel Adams and other Whig leaders were dismayed. Just a month before, the Boston crowd had demonstrated its capacity for restraint. While destroying the tea, the crowd had acted in defense of public liberties, and without hostility. Now the townspeople had demonstrated their capacity for cruelty. While tormenting Malcom, the crowd had acted in revenge for private wrongs, and with extreme violence. Patriot organizers recognized that the Malcom incident could only damage Boston's reputation and hurt the popular cause. In the pages of the *Boston Gazette* and the *Massachusetts Spy,* they were quick to blame Malcom for his own mistreatment and to disavow the assault together. Privately, they agreed that the time had come for Boston to adopt a more moderate form of resistance.

Samuel Adams, in the meantime, would not let this nasty affair detract from the glorious destruction of the tea. In the House of Representatives, he continued to capitalize on Whig enthusiasm, much to the disadvantage of local Tories. In February, Adams collaborated with his cousin, John, and a fellow Patriot, Joseph Hawley, to impeach the chief justice of the Superior Court, Peter Oliver. Peter was the brother of Andrew Oliver, the Stamp Act Commissioner who had suffered so greatly at the hands of the Sons of Liberty. Peter was also one of the judges who agreed to accept his salary from the Crown, rather than from the colonial treasury. For this crime, Adams and his friends in the House determined that he was unfit for service. By a vote of 92 to 8, the House impeached the chief justice. Though the impeachment was not legally binding unless acted upon by Governor Hutchinson, who of course refused to sanction Adams's antics, patriotic jurymen nevertheless refused to sit in Oliver's court.

Adams also worked to keep the people zealous for the popular cause, though not so zealous that they might riot. He served on a town committee that selected John Hancock to deliver that year's Massacre Oration, an annual commemoration during which the murderous Redcoats were once again vilified and their victims once again made martyrs. Though wealthy and popular, Hancock was neither an accomplished writer nor an experienced orator. The Massacre oration was, in fact, one of his first public addresses. But Adams worked with Hancock for weeks in preparation. Adams himself was rumored to have written Hancock's speech, and he solicited the Reverend Samuel Cooper to coach Hancock on his presentation. The oration had its desired effect. Delivered before an audience that filled the Old South, the eulogy was met with "universal applause" and, as John Adams recounted, "exceeded the expectations of everybody." So moving was the speech that upon its conclusion the members of the audience spontaneously began to

This cartoon depicts the Sons of Liberty as violent brutes. One Liberty Boy brandishes a club; others force their feathered victim to drink tea. A noose hangs ominously from the Liberty Tree while, in the background, patriots dump tea overboard.

donate sums for those persons who had been wounded during the massacre.

Adams must have been gratified with the progress of events. During the previous winter, the popular party appeared on the verge of collapse. Now it suddenly seemed full of life and vigor. Except for a small clique of Hutchinson's friends, the people and politicians of Boston stood firmly behind the Whig party. The committees of correspondence were well organized, and as a result, much of the Massachusetts countryside supported the Whigs as well. Everywhere Adams turned he was met with patriotic fervor. The citizens of New England, Adams reported, "are united and resolute."

As winter turned to spring, though, there began to develop beneath this resolution a sense of anxiety. King George and his ministers were certain to be angry about the colonists' flagrant destruction of the tea. The East India Company was clamoring for restitution of the £18,000 of inventory it had lost. One patriot on a visit to London reported speaking with two members of Parliament who, though "well meaning Men & friends to America," nevertheless believed that "any thing short of hanging us & battering down our Towns, is perfect Lenity." Given such sentiment, it was only a matter of time before Parliament would respond. But when? And with what degree of severity?

March passed, and even April, and yet no word arrived from England. Some Bostonians began to worry, and a few even suggested that the town should pay for the tea. Samuel Adams cringed at this suggestion and the cowardice behind it. It was Governor Hutchinson, Adams observed, who by refusing to grant the *Dartmouth*'s return "both encouragd & provoked the people to destroy the Tea." Viewed in such a light, "the Question is easily decided who ought in Justice to pay for the Tea, if it ought to be paid for at all." But even Samuel Adams must have begun to grow nervous with anticipation. His cousin, John, did. He waited in vain for news to arrive from England. By April's end John could only lament, "Still! Silent as midnight!"

When, on May 10, news of Parliament's reaction finally did arrive, it stunned the people of Boston. The first punitive lash, known as the Port Bill, imposed a blockade on Boston Harbor; after June 1, no ship would be allowed to enter or leave the port. This piece of legislation put Boston in an economic stranglehold. From the wealthiest merchant down to the poorest apprentice, the people's livelihood depended on their maritime trade. By cutting Boston off from the Atlantic world, the Port Bill meant certain destitution. But that was precisely what Lord North intended.

To enforce the blockade, he ordered a small fleet of warships to keep watch over the bay. In mid-May these ships began to arrive; one of them carried General Thomas Gage, the commander of British forces in America. Gage had been sent to serve as governor in the place of Thomas Hutchinson, who for months had requested relief from his duties. After decades of doing battle with the Adamses and Otises, after having his house broken to pieces by the mob, after suffering the humiliating publication of his private papers, Hutchinson at last succumbed.

Boston Patriots, consumed with the shock of the Port Bill, found little time to savor Hutchinson's defeat. And as harsh as the Port Bill was, it was only just the beginning of Boston's penalty. General Gage had orders to relocate the General Court to Salem, far from the reach of Boston's Sons of Liberty. Additionally, Parliament passed the Massachusetts Government Act, which radically transformed the colony's charter.

From that time on, the governor would have the power to appoint his own councilors, rather than selecting from those nominated by the House. The governor was also given the power to appoint judges, and juries would now be empanelled by the sheriff. Most significant, though, the Massachusetts Government Act severely restricted the Boston town meeting. For over a century, the town meeting had been the forum in which New Englanders met to debate issues, forge consensus, and develop policy; it was the very arena in which Samuel Adams had made his first mark on Massachusetts politics. Most Bostonians would not so much as cry "Liberty!" without first putting it up for vote in the town meeting, but now under the Government Act, the town was restricted to one meeting per year and was bound to adhere to a limited agenda pertaining only to local affairs.

Nor was this the end of the sanctions placed on Boston. The Quartering Act authorized General Gage to seize empty buildings for the billeting of British troops, and the Administration of Justice Act decreed that royal officers accused of crimes would be prosecuted in England rather than in Massachusetts. There would be no more massacre trials.

Known variously as the Coercive Acts or the Intolerable Acts, these punitive measures created an uproar in the American colonies. Not even the most ardent American Tories expected Parliament to respond so harshly to the destruction of the tea. Samuel Adams, on the other hand, may have. For several years he had prodded the people of Massachusetts. He watched with dismay as their resoluteness ebbed and flowed in response to the cycles of British taxation. He yearned for the day when New Englanders would overcome their complacency and at long last commit themselves to the cause of liberty. By dumping the tea they had done just that. They had cast their lots together and surrendered themselves to the retribution that was bound to come.

That retribution played right into Adams's hands. Within days after the Port Bill arrived, Adams had scratched off letters to the committees of correspondence throughout Massachusetts, and to his friends in London, New York, and Philadelphia. In response, expressions of sympathy poured in from the various colonies. Outrage was the universal reaction to the Intolerable Acts, and Patriots from all along the Atlantic seaboard promised to share in Boston's plight.

The town of Marblehead, 15 miles north, offered Boston merchants the use of its docks and warehouses; in Philadelphia, the Sons of Liberty collected donations for those Bostonians who lost their income because of the blockade; and in Virginia, the House of Burgesses declared a day of "fasting, humiliation, and prayer" on behalf of the oppressed citizens of New England. To Adams's delight, "The Boston Port bill suddenly wrought a Union of the Colonies which could not be brot about by the Industry of years."

Determined to make the most of this sudden union, Adams attempted once again to revive interest in his scheme of nonimportation. But he had learned from the

After Parliament closed the port of Boston, Samuel Adams wrote to Ezekiel Williams of Wethersfield, Connecticut, to express his gratitude to the town for its generous donation of wheat, rye, and corn to the citizens of Boston, "now Suffering the Stroke of Ministerial Vengeance as they apprehend, for the Liberties of America."

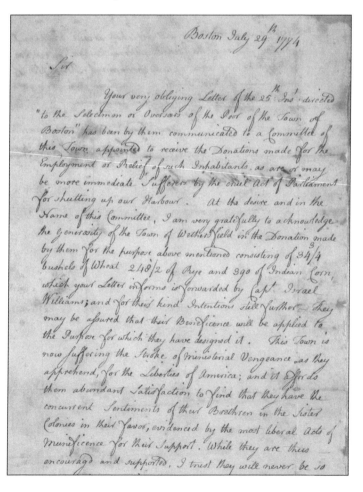

mistakes of his earlier, futile efforts. Rather than appeal to the coastal merchants, who were far too dependent on English trade to support a boycott, Adams first turned to the mechanics and farmers living in the New England countryside. Through the various committees of correspondence, Adams circulated an agreement known as the Solemn League and Covenant. Unlike his previous plan, which depended on merchants not to import British goods, the Solemn League depended on the people of New England neither to buy British goods, nor to sell their wares and produce for distribution overseas. The Solemn League in essence demanded a virtual halt to all commerce with Britain, and in the rural areas of the colony it was greeted with much enthusiasm.

As Adams had predicted, however, the Boston merchants were much less willing to cooperate. Faced with the very real possibility of financial disaster, many pleaded for milder measures, and hoped to effect a reconciliation with England. Only after several weeks of heated opposition did they at last acquiesce to Adams's plan. Equally lukewarm was the response of New York merchants, who promised only to consider the Solemn League at some point in the future. Instead, the New Yorkers proposed, and other colonies agreed, that the best course of action might be another congress, much like the Stamp Act Congress. Such an assembly would afford the colonists the opportunity to share their opinions on the state of colonial affairs, and perhaps to devise some sort of unified response to Parliament's latest impositions.

Adams begrudgingly received this proposal. Though he had in previous years favored the idea of a congress, he now believed that the time was ripe for action. A congress promised nothing but debate and deliberation, at most a few strongly worded resolutions that inevitably would fall upon deaf ears. Yet Adams recognized that he could not let the opportunity slip by, nor could he entrust this important work to others. On June 17, Adams stood before the House of Representatives, which was then convened in its new Salem home, and ordered that the public be cleared from the chamber. After the room had been emptied of all but his fellow delegates, Adams bolted the chamber door and hid the key in his pocket. Over the next few hours, the House compiled a series of resolutions in protest of the Coercive Acts.

When General Gage got wind that the House had closed its session, he knew that Adams was up to no good, and he sent his secretary with orders to dissolve the assembly. Furiously, the secretary pounded on the chamber door. He even read the general's order aloud, but the House would not disband. Instead, the representatives heard nominations for delegates to represent Massachusetts in the upcoming congress. With little deliberation they elected a five-man slate. Along with Robert Treat Paine, Thomas Cushing, James Bowdoin, and his cousin John, Samuel Adams was bound for the Continental Congress in Philadelphia.

All at once, the pace of events began to accelerate. The congress was scheduled to meet in early September, which left Adams little time to prepare for the journey. Never in his life had he traveled so far from home, and he did not know for certain how long he would be away. He first met with Boston's leading Patriots, Dr. Joseph Warren in particular, to ensure that the Whig party would stay the course during his absence. He then attended to his wife, Betsy, who assured him that she could manage their household just fine while he was away. Having satisfied himself that all was in order, Adams felt ready for his departure. But there remained one piece of unfinished business.

In early August, a little more than a week before he planned to depart, Adams was distracted from his supper by a knock on his door. A fashionable tailor was calling, and though he would not say why he was there or who had sent him, the tailor insisted on taking Adams's measurements. Afterwards, the tailor departed, but no sooner had the family returned to their meal than they were again interrupted by a knock. This time it was a hatter, who proceeded to measure Adams's head but who, like the tailor, refused to divulge the nature of his visit. The hatter was then followed by a shoemaker, every bit as secretive as his predecessors. Several other outfitters waited on Adams that night, and when they had finally gone, his family was left only to speculate on this curious event.

A few days later the mystery was solved when a trunk arrived at Adams's door. As Adams's daughter later remembered, the aging patriot opened the trunk to find "a complete suit of clothes, two pairs of shoes of the best style, a set of silver shoe-buckles, a set of gold knee-buckles, a set of gold sleeve-buttons, an elegant cocked hat, a gold-headed cane, a red cloak, and a number of minor articles of wearing-apparel." This new wardrobe was a gift from the Sons of Liberty, who in part wanted to thank Adams for his years of devoted service, but who also wanted to make sure that Adams did not arrive in Philadelphia dressed in the tattered old clothes he had worn for so many years.

On August 10, a nattily attired Samuel Adams and his fellow delegates departed for Philadelphia. Riding in a four-horse coach, and accompanied by six armed and mounted servants, the delegates traveled in high style. Along the way they made stops in Connecticut, New York, and New Jersey, where they were entertained by the Sons of Liberty. Church bells pealed as the procession rode into view, and cannon fired in their honor. "No governor of a province," John Adams declared, "nor general of any army was ever treated with so much ceremony." The gentlemen at last arrived in Philadelphia, and though "dirty, dusty, and fatigued," they made haste for the City Tavern, "the most genteel one in America," where they were introduced to the delegates from the other colonies. Here in Philadelphia were fifty-six of America's leading men. Many of them had served on their local committees of correspondence, almost half were lawyers, and virtually all had sat in their respective colonial legislatures.

For Samuel Adams the experience must have been very awkward. His reputation as a foremost radical had proceeded him, and his fellow delegates were certain to scrutinize the "great incendiary." But Adams was unaccustomed to such attention. It was one thing for him to moderate a town meeting, surrounded by his friends and neighbors, but quite another to stand before the likes of John Dickinson or George Washington. Never a great orator, Adams lacked the refinement and polish of an elite colonial gentleman. But Adams was little concerned with what these men thought of his breeding or manners. He was much more concerned with what they thought of his politics.

In New York, while en route to the congress, Adams had been warned by several Patriots that some of the conservative delegates feared he was too radical and were likely to shy away from any drastic proposals. To counter this perception, Adams and his fellow Massachusetts delegates agreed to present themselves as moderately as possible. They resolved to "to act with great delicacy and caution, to keep ourselves out of sight, and to feel pulses, and to sound the depths," rather than to overwhelm the other delegations with radical schemes.

Early in the congress, the Massachusetts delegates found an opportunity to prove their moderation. On the second day, Thomas Cushing proposed that the session be opened with a prayer, but some delegates objected. John Jay of New York observed that the congress "was so divided in religious Sentiments, some Episcopalians, some Quakers, some anabaptists, some Presbyterians and some Congregationalists," that the delegates would never agree on "the same Act of Worship."

Samuel Adams, however, recognized that many of the Virginia and Carolina delegates were members of the Church of England, and he saw his chance to earn their esteem. Adams was renowned for his ardent Congregationalism. At one time Adams had written in the Boston newspapers against an American episcopacy. But now he rose to declare that "he was no bigot, and could hear a prayer from a gentleman of piety and virtue, who was at the same time a friend to his country." Adams then nominated the prominent Philadelphia Anglican clergyman, Jacob Duché, to say the prayer. By so doing, Adams endeared himself to the Southern delegates, and convinced many others that he was not the violent extremist they had taken him for. John Adams was delighted by his cousin's "Masterly stroke of policy."

In debates, too, the Massachusetts delegates continued to proceed reservedly. It soon became apparent that the congress was divided into two camps. All agreed that the Coercive Acts were unacceptable, but the delegates differed as to what course of action the colonists should take. Samuel Adams, of course, favored staunch resistance. He found strong allies in the Patriots of Virginia, such as Richard Henry Lee. Adams met privately with the Virginia representatives, and through them many of his ideas were introduced to congress. So radical were the delegates from the "Old Dominion" that one Pennsylvania commentator observed, "Next to the Virginians, the Bostonians are mere Milksops."

In contrast to the radical coalition that formed around the Massachusetts and Virginia delegates was a more moderate faction spearheaded by Joseph Galloway of Pennsylvania, and James Duane and John Jay of New York. Galloway

EXTRACTS

FROM THE

VOTES and PROCEEDINGS

Of the AMERICAN CONTINENTAL

CONGRESS,

Held at PHILADELPHIA on the

5th of *September* 1774.

CONTAINING

The BILL of RIGHTS, a Lift of GRIEV-
ANCES, Occafional Refolves, the
Affociation, an *Addrefs* to the PEOPLE
of GREAT-BRITAIN, and a *Memorial*
to the INHABITANTS of the BRITISH
AMERICAN COLONIES.

Publifhed by order of the CONGRESS.

PHILADELPHIA:

Printed by WILLIAM and THOMAS BRADFORD,
October 27*th,* M,DCC,LXXIV.

Before adjourning in October 1774, the First Continental Congress ordered the publication of its most important resolutions, including the Articles of Association, an agreement to cease trade with Great Britain until the colonists' grievances were addressed.

spoke for many of the moderates when he expressed his desire to "bring about a Reconciliation between the two Countries upon Principles of Liberty and Government." He must have had Samuel Adams in mind when he complained that reconciliation would be made difficult by "the Violent Temper of the Warm & indiscreet People here."

For more than a week the congress deliberated, and it appeared that the two factions might deadlock. But Samuel Adams had prepared for such a contingency. Before leaving Massachusetts he had met with Dr. Joseph Warren and drawn up plans for a meeting of the residents of Suffolk County, in lieu of the outlawed Boston town meeting. Adams instructed Warren to foment opposition to General Gage and the Intolerable Acts, to push the Suffolk County meeting toward headstrong resistance, and to keep Adams apprised of his progress. "Continual expresses were employed between Philadelphia and Boston," observed Joseph Galloway. "By one of these expresses came the inflammatory resolves of the county of Suffolk." Delivered by the silversmith and noted Patriot Paul Revere, the Suffolk Resolves proclaimed that the Coercive Acts were unconstitutional, urged the citizens of Massachusetts to withhold taxes until those acts were repealed, encouraged the formation of militias, and proposed economic sanctions against Britain.

For Galloway, these resolves amounted to nothing less than "a complete declaration of war against Great-Britain." But, as Adams had hoped, the other congressional delegates were taken by the New Englanders' courage and determination. They sympathized with the plight of Massachusetts, now strangling in the iron grip of the blockade, and they agreed, as John Adams recounted, to "support Massachusetts or perish with her."

To the dismay of the moderate faction, the Continental Congress endorsed the Suffolk Resolves on September 17. Subsequently, the congress fell under the sway of the more radical faction. On September 28, the delegates voted to table Galloway's Plan of Union with Great Britain, effectively killing that conciliatory proposal. Three weeks later, the congress voted to adopt a nonimportation and nonexportation agreement known as the Association, which was loosely based on the boycott strategy that Adams had promoted for years. Before it adjourned, the congress also ratified a Declaration of Rights, approved an address to the citizens of Quebec that urged Canadians to ally themselves with the colonies, and agreed to reconvene in May 1775, unless the colonists' grievances were redressed by that time. In late October, Adams returned to Massachusetts very pleased with what he had accomplished. The congress had exceeded his greatest expectations, conducting all of its business "perfectly to his liking as if he were [its] sole director."

8

IS NOT AMERICA
ALREADY
INDEPENDENT?

Though he had been away at the Continental Congress for only three months, much had changed in Samuel Adams's hometown during that time. Tories seeking refuge from the Whig-dominated countryside had begun to trickle into Boston. Redcoats marched through the streets in numbers not seen since the massacre, and several British men-of-war, their guns fixed on the town, loomed ominously over the bay. Yet the people of Massachusetts remained steadfast even in the face of such military force. Early in October, General Gage decided not to convene the General Court, but the representatives to that body gathered against his orders. Calling itself the Provincial Congress, this assembly chose John Hancock to serve as its president, and Samuel Adams, in absentia, to serve as its secretary. It further organized a Committee of Safety, whose purpose was to make ready for the colony's defense. Through the winter, the people of New England collected arms and ammunition; there seemed little doubt in their minds that the crisis would soon be upon them.

In the meantime, Whig leaders endeavored to keep the people's spirit high. On March 5, 1775, Dr. Joseph Warren delivered the annual Boston Massacre oration before a rapt

audience. As the author of the Suffolk Resolves, it was fitting he should make the speech. For the occasion Warren
donned a classical toga, reminiscent of a Greek or Roman
statesman, and he held a white handkerchief in his hand as
if the thought of the massacre victims might reduce him to
tears. From this morale-boosting oration, Hancock and
Adams returned to the Provincial Congress in Concord.
Despite rumors that Gage was plotting for their arrest, the
two stouthearted leaders continued to prepare for an armed
conflict. The Provincial Congress published rules and regulations for the Massachusetts army, and it ordered local
towns to ready their militia. Samuel Adams also headed a
committee that sought to form a military alliance with the
Mohawk Indians living in northwestern New England.

General Gage began to worry. Like most British strate-
gists, he doubted that the Americans could long defend
themselves against his well-equipped veteran troops. Yet the
colonists had managed to amass a disquietingly large quantity
of munitions. More frustrating than the colonists' arms,
though, was their attitude. That preparing for war against
the mother country amounted to treason was a fact the
Patriots seemed to have forgotten. Gage resolved to remind
the colonists of their proper place. In mid-April 1775, the
general received orders from London to quash the incipient
rebellion, and he determined to march on Concord and
seize the military stores accumulated there.

Gage soon learned the folly of marching into a countryside controlled by the militias of Massachusetts. Boston
Patriots quickly discovered his plan, and dispatched Paul
Revere and William Dawes to warn the Minutemen. Just
after daybreak on the morning of April 19, British troops
under the command of Major John Pitcairn encountered the
Lexington militia on the green near Munroe's Tavern.
Pitcairn ordered his soldiers to surround and disarm the
militiamen, and in the ensuing commotion, a shot was
fired. Whether a British or American soldier first pulled the

trigger remains unclear, but in the skirmish that followed, eight Americans were killed.

The Lexington militia fell back, and Pitcairn's regulars regrouped. The Redcoats then marched on to Concord to rejoin forces with Lieutenant Colonel Francis Smith and to destroy several cannon pieces collected there. At the North Bridge, near the conjunction of the Concord and Assabet Rivers, the British troops again confronted American volunteers. The Minutemen held their position, though, and when the column advanced, they opened fire. After suffering more than a dozen casualties, Smith and his troops withdrew.

The countryside was now filled with American volunteers, and the British officers recognized the danger they were in. There was only one road back to Boston, and it was flanked by New England riflemen. Smith had no choice but to order a brisk retreat to Boston, and it was then that the rout began. American sharpshooters took cover behind thickets, trees, and barns, and the retreating Redcoats made easy targets. By day's end, almost 300 British soldiers, nearly

Taking cover behind trees, hills, and stone walls, Massachusetts marksmen killed or wounded nearly 300 British troops as they hastily retreated to Boston. According to American accounts, the Redcoats set fire to local buildings and shops, seen here burning in the distance.

a third of Smith's fighting force, lay dead or wounded. The first battle of the American Revolution was a decided victory for the militias of Massachusetts.

Samuel Adams and John Hancock, meanwhile, made haste to elude the British scouts. At Philadelphia, the Sons of Liberty coordinated another gallant reception for the Massachusetts heroes, consisting of, as one loyalist remembered "two or three hundred gentlemen on horseback, preceded, however by the newly chosen city military officers, two and two with drawn swords, followed by John Hancock and Samuel Adams in a phaeton and pair." Church bells once again announced the delegates' arrival and town folk lined the streets to catch a glimpse of the famous Patriots who had just barely escaped General Gage's platoons. At the Second Continental Congress, too, the Massachusetts delegates found that the victories at Lexington and Concord greatly improved their stature. Shortly after the assembly convened, President Peyton Randolph was recalled to Virginia, and the delegates elected John Hancock to serve in his absence.

For the next several months, the congress busied itself with making provisions for a defensive war. On May 18, the assembly received news that Ethan Allen and Benedict Arnold had captured the British Fort Ticonderoga on Lake Champlain. A few weeks later the representatives agreed to organize a Continental Army. The Massachusetts delegation would have preferred to appoint a New Englander to command the army; John Hancock longed for the post. But the Adams cousins recognized the ongoing need to build coalitions and to assure their countryman that the crisis with England was not simply a Massachusetts affair.

In early June, after much consultation with his cousin Samuel, John Adams proposed that a Virginian, Colonel George Washington, who had first tasted battle during the French and Indian War, assume leadership over the Continental Army. A few days later, the Congress unanimously elected Washington commander in chief, much to Hancock's dismay. The martial spirit continued to guide congressional affairs, and by summer's end, the delegates had approved an invasion of Canada, published a *Declaration on Taking Arms*, and agreed to establish a system of military hospitals.

Samuel Adams knew that such steps ultimately would lead to independence, but he began to grow impatient with the congress's delay. To make matters worse, Adams began to receive troubling news from home. After defeat at Lexington and Concord, General Cage had tightened his grip on Boston. On June 12, Gage offered amnesty to "all persons who shall forthwith lay down their arms." But he excluded from this pardon "Samuel Adams and John Hancock, whose offences are of too flagitious a nature to admit of any other consideration than that of condign punishment."

That same day the general imposed martial law, putting the town at the mercy of the 3,500 Redcoats garrisoned there. The beloved Old South, the very meeting house that had swelled with anticipation before the Boston Tea Party, was now converted into a stable for British horses. Many residents were forced to flee Boston, their houses given over to British officers. Samuel Adams must have cringed to think that Redcoats now lived in his house. But he was much more concerned for his son, who was trapped in Boston, and for his wife, who was forced to relocate the family.

More bleak news reached Adams in late June. Earlier that month, American forces under the command of General Israel Putnam marched on Bunker Hill in Charlestown. From that hill the British fortifications in Boston were vulnerable to artillery fire, as were naval vessels in port, and the British intended to take the hill so as to strengthen their hold on the town. After American spies learned of this plan, General Putnam decided to make a preemptive strike. On June 16, under cover of night, Putnam's troops began to dig in.

At dawn they discovered they had made a costly mistake. They had built their fortifications not on Bunker Hill, but on Breed's Hill, which was smaller, and in closer range

CHARLES TOWN

BOSTON

to British cannon. At that point, little could be done to correct the error. British General William Howe had already ordered an attack on the American position. The battle lasted long into the day. British artillery fired incendiary bombs into Charlestown, leaving the town in flames. Twice the Redcoats charged up Breed's Hill and twice they were repelled. American forces grew low on ammunition, however, and though Dr. Joseph Warren, now a major general in the Massachusetts militia, had brought reinforcements from Charlestown, they too had a short supply of powder and balls. As the regulars prepared for a third charge, Colonel William Prescott issued his famous order, "Don't shoot till you see the whites of their eyes!" But on their third attempt, the British soldiers finally captured the hill and compelled American forces to retreat.

text continues on page 134

On June 17, 1775, British General William Howe awoke to discover that, in the middle of the night, American forces had begun building fortifications on the hills overlooking Charlestown. Howe immediately ordered his troops to launch an assault. While the battle raged, British shells engulfed Charlestown in flames.

131

An Easy, Genteel Figure

While returning to the Second Continental Congress after a brief adjournment in September 1775, John Adams taught Samuel how to ride a horse. In the following letter, John tells of Samuel's efforts, of the discomfort that he suffered, and of his ultimate success. (The President whom John mentions is John Hancock, President of the Continental Congress. The Secretary is Samuel Adams, the Massachusetts Secretary of State.) More poignant than the story John tells, however, was the fact that the letter was written to James Warren. Warren's brother, Joseph, was recently killed in the Battle of Bunker Hill, and it may be that John sent this humorous letter to boost Warren's spirit.

Dr Sir   Philadelphia Septr. 17. 1775

You know the aversion, which your Secretary has ever entertained to riding, on Horseback. He never would be perswaded to mount a Horse. The last time we were here, I often laboured to perswade him, for the Sake of his Health, but in vain. Soon after We Sat out, on the last Journey, I reflected that Some Degree of Skill and Dexterity in Horsemanship, was necessary to the Character of a Statesman. It would take more Time and Paper than I have to Spare, to shew the Utility of Horsemanship to a Politician; So I shall take this for granted. But I pointed out the particulars to him, and likewise shewed him that Sociability would be greatly promoted, by his mounting one of my Horses.

On Saturday the second day of September 1775, in the Town of Grafton He was prevailed on to put my Servant with his, into Harrisons Chaise and to mount upon my Horse, a very genteel, and easy little Creature. We were all disappointed and Surprised.... We beheld, an easy, genteel Figure, upon the Horse, and a good deal of Spirit and facility, in the Management of the Horse, insomuch that We soon found our Servants were making Some disagreable Comparisons, and Since our arrival here I am told that Fessenden (impudent Scoundrel!) reports that the Secretary rides fifty per Cent better than your Correspondent.

In this manner, We rode to Woodstock, where we put up for the Sabbath. It was Soon observed that the Secretary, could not Sit So erect in his Chair as he had Sat upon his Horse, but Seemed to be neither sensible of the Disease or the Remedy. I Soon perceived and apprised him of both. On Sunday Evening, at Mr Dexters, where we drank Coffee & Spent an agreable Evening I perswaded him to purchase two yards of flannell which we carried to our Landlady, who with the assistance of a Tayler Woman in the House, made up a Pair of Drawers, which the next Morning were put on, and not only defended the Secretary from any further Injury, but entirely healed the little Breach which had been begun.

Still an Imperfection remained. Our Secretary had not yet learned to mount and dismount. Two Servants were necessary to attend upon these Occasions, one to hold the Bridle and Stirrup, the other to boost the Secretary. This was rather a ridiculous Circumstance Still. At last, I undertook to instruct him the necessary Art of mounting. . . . I taught him to grasp the Bridle, with his Right Hand over the Pummell of his Saddle, to place his left Foot firm in the Stirrup; to twist his left Hand into the Horses Main, about half Way between his Ears and his Shoulders, and then a vigorous Exertion of his Strength would carry him very gracefully into the Seat, without the least Danger of falling over on [the] other Side. The Experiment was tryed and Succeeded to Admiration.

Thus equipped and instructed, our Horseman rode all the Way from Woodstock to Philadelphia, Sometimes upon one of my Horses, Sometimes on the other-and acquired fresh Strength, Courage, Activity and Spirit every day. His Health is much improved by it, and I value myself, very much upon the Merit of having probably added Several Years, to a Life So important to his Country, by the little Pains I took to perswade him to mount and teach him to ride.

text continued from page 131

Though a strategic defeat, Bunker Hill represented a moral victory for the colonists. The New England soldiers had inflicted heavy casualties on the Redcoats—more than a thousand British troops were killed or wounded—and they had demonstrated that they could fight against any professional army. Adams rejoiced at his countrymen's valor, but he was greatly afflicted by the news that his "truly amiable and worthy Friend," Joseph Warren, had been killed during the Redcoats' final charge. Adams found solace in the fact that Warren had fallen "in the glorious Struggle for the publick Liberty."

However, little could assuage his concern about his wife and family. "It is painful to me," Adams wrote Betsy, "to reflect upon the Terror I must suppose you were under on hearing the Noise of War so near you." On August 11, to Adams's great relief, the congress agreed to a one-month recess. Weary and homesick, Adams journeyed back to Massachusetts. Though he could never go home—not so long as Boston remained under siege—it was enough for Adams to return to his family, who had fled west to Watertown. He was delighted to be with his wife again, and equally delighted to learn that his son, Samuel, had accepted a surgeon's position in the army.

The respite served Adams well. In September, he once again made the trip to Philadelphia, but with more energy and robustness than before. At cousin John's suggestion, Samuel even took the opportunity to learn to ride a horse, because, as the younger Adams explained, "Some Degree of Skill and Dexterity in Horsemanship, was necessary to the Character of a Statesman."

In the months that followed, Adams's renewed vitality was put to the test. Perhaps more than any other delegate, Adams returned to the Continental Congress ready to sever ties with Great Britain. With his home under siege, his family forced to flee, and his friends killed in battle, the very notion of dependence seemed a farce. "Can Nations at War," Adams demanded to know, "be said to be dependent either upon the other?" This was a question, however, that the other delegates to congress were slow to answer. Most recognized, at least privately, that the war in New England dashed any real possibility of reconciliation. Yet notwithstanding the fact that King George had on August 23 declared the colonies to be in a state of "open and avowed rebellion," few American leaders were prepared to make the unfathomable breach. In 1775, the historical, cultural, and familial bonds with England were too firm, the future of America too uncertain, and the prospect of failure too horrific for the colonies to declare their independence.

Instead, the moderate faction in congress followed the lead of John Dickinson, the author of the famous *Letters of a Farmer in Pennsylvania*. First published in 1768, these letters decried taxation without representation, and they established Dickinson as a foremost defender of American liberties. But Dickinson believed that those liberties could best be preserved through a negotiated settlement with the mother country, and he endeavored to push the congress in that direction. Much to the dismay of Samuel and John Adams, who in private circles spoke ill of his moderate clique, Dickinson ardently promoted the Olive Branch Petition, a proclamation of allegiance to the king. Further, he threatened to withdraw from the congress if the Massachusetts delegates stood in his way.

However much Samuel Adams might have relished the idea of beleaguered New England fighting alone for the valiant cause of freedom, he was far too realistic to embrace it. And so, he continued to bide his time and work indirectly for independence. His strategy was to urge the various colonies to write new constitutions and open trade with foreign nations. In November the congress authorized New Hampshire to establish a new government; in December it instructed Virginia to do the same. Adams predicted that other colonies would soon follow suit. "When this is done," Adams wrote, "the Colonies will feel their Independence—the Way will be prepared for a Confederation, and one Government may be formd with the Consent of the whole."

In the meantime, Adams was pleased to observe that the course of military events also pointed toward a final break with Britain. Throughout the winter months, the Continental Congress continued to prepare for an extended armed conflict, negotiating for the purchase of military supplies abroad, authorizing the construction of ships for the Continental Navy, and developing various regulations for soldiers, privateers, and prisoners of war. In mid-January the Congress received word that General Richard Montgomery's assault on Quebec had been repulsed and Montgomery mortally wounded, and it immediately ordered reinforcements to the Canadian front.

Samuel Adams struggled to endure the incessant delay. For a while he sustained himself with the belief "that what I most earnestly wish for will in due time be effected." In the early months of 1776, several events transpired to justify Adams's faith. On January 10, Thomas Paine anonymously published the pamphlet, *Common Sense*. Unlike the various legal discourses written in defense of the American cause, or the many tracts that recalled the classical republicanism of ancient Rome, *Common Sense* was written in plain language, with logic that appealed to ordinary folk. Railing against "the Royal Brute of Britain," Paine urged, "O ye that love mankind! Ye that dare oppose, not only the tyranny, but the tyrant, stand forth!" *Common Sense*

This Massachusetts three-shilling note was printed by Paul Revere in 1775. It depicts an armed American holding the Magna Carta. The Latin inscription reads: By arms he seeks peace with freedom.

immediately sold 120,000 copies, and did more to turn American opinion toward independence than any other pamphlet.

In Philadelphia, the delegates sensed the shift in public sentiment, and their reticence began to dissolve. Two months later, their revolutionary mettle was further strengthened by the military success of George Washington. On the dark night of March 4, Continental soldiers commanded by Washington's artillery chief, Colonel Henry Knox, secretly dragged 55 cannons to the top of Dorchester Heights, a promontory to the south of Boston. From these heights Washington's guns could easily bombard British fortifications in the town, as well as the men-of-war anchored in the harbor.

The next morning, exactly six years to the day after the Boston Massacre, General Howe discovered Washington's feat. He had no choice but to abandon the town. On March 17, after an occupation that had lasted well over a year, British troops evacuated Boston, and the town was finally returned to the people of Massachusetts. Adams was exultant that his home had at last been rescued from the "savage Troops," and now more than ever he craved a separation from Britain. "Is not America already independent?" he asked. "Why then not declare it?"

In May, word arrived from England that King George was negotiating for the enlistment of 17,000 German mercenaries to suppress the American rebellion. Even the congress's more conciliatory members were forced to admit that this was not the act of a monarch who hoped for peace. Two weeks later the congress received Richard Henry Lee's resolution in favor of independence. It then appointed a committee, consisting of Thomas Jefferson, John Adams, Benjamin Franklin, Roger Sherman, and Robert Livingston, to draft a declaration. On June 28, the committee's draft was read before congress, and after a few days of debate, the congress declared that the colonies "are, and of Right ought to be FREE AND INDEPENDENT STATES."

On June 10, 1776, the Continental Congress appointed Thomas Jefferson, John Adams, Benjamin Franklin, Roger Sherman, and Robert Livingston to write the Declaration of Independence. Jefferson penned most of the document, and his fellow committeemen offered numerous minor revisions. The Congress declared Independence on July 2 and adopted the formal Declaration two days later.

9

THE STORM IS NOW OVER

The Declaration of Independence represented in many ways the culmination of Samuel Adams's life work. For three decades he had labored to free the people of Massachusetts from the yoke of imperial opression. As a writer of newspaper articles, as the head of the Caucus Club, as the moderator of town meetings, and as clerk of the House of Representatives, Adams tirelessly endeavored to thwart the royal governors he believed to be corrupt and to protest the taxation he believed to be unconstitutional.

Through the long struggle Adams may not have always understood that resistance would ultimately lead to rebellion. During the Sugar and Stamp Act crises there seemed no reason to think that the preservation of American liberties would necessitate dissolution of the British Empire. But as the conflict escalated, Adams became appalled at the lengths to which the royal administration was willing to go to keep the colonies in submission. The quartering of troops in Boston, which erupted in such hostile and horrific bloodshed during the massacre, and the closure of the port, which reduced Adams's neighbors to poverty, convinced the aging Patriot that a break with England would have to come.

Ironically, though, Adams's role within the Continental Congress began to diminish after the colonies had taken the "decisive Step" of independence. His strengths lay in the instigation of resistance rather than in the administration of revolution. Adams had little of the training, and none of the polish, necessary for a career in foreign diplomacy. And though he had been the guiding force behind nonimportation and nonexportation, Adams knew little about the new nation's wartime economic needs. He continued to serve on a multitude of minor committees, but as John Adams recorded, "Samuel spoke but rarely in Congress, and never entered into any extensive Arguments."

When he did speak, Adams's lack of expertise often revealed itself. For example, though he possessed virtually no military experience, Adams was far too concerned with the outcome of the war not to meddle in the army's affairs. His naïveté became apparent in the early phases of the conflict. He initially opposed the idea of a standing army of professional soldiers, instead favoring a militia of volunteer citizens. In part because he had suffered through the encampment of Redcoats in Boston and in part because he had studied the works of English republican writers, Adams believed that standing armies "were always dangerous to the Liberties of the People." As he explained to his friend James Warren, "Men who have been long subject to military Laws and inured to military Customs and Habits, may lose the Spirit and Feeling of Citizens."

Even after Adams's fellow delegates had convinced him that the various local militias were too diffuse, too unregulated, and too unreliable to defeat well-organized veteran British soldiers, he continued to argue that the army should ultimately be answerable only to the civilian congress. Not until December 1776, after General Howe's army had crossed the Hudson and begun its march toward Philadelphia, did Adams begrudgingly acquiesce to the expansion of General Washington's authority.

Adams further complicated the war effort by meddling in the appointment of officers. The "great incendiary" ardently wished for American victories. Failure, Adams believed, resulted from a weakness of will, and he was quick to blame American generals when their armies were defeated. For instance, Adams quickly lost patience with General Philip Schuyler, Commander of the Northern Army. On New Year's Eve, 1775, Schuyler's forces attacked Quebec, but were easily repelled from the fortified city.

Adams had long wished for the liberation of Canada, and shortly after Schuyler's defeat, he began privately to advocate the general's removal. In Schuyler's stead, Adams hoped to promote General Horatio Gates, a native Englishman who nevertheless managed to impress the Massachusetts delegates and their allies with his strict deference to congressional authority. Gates's accomplishments were limited, but his confidence was boundless, and Adams was taken by his zeal. In January 1777, Adams reported to his cousin, John, that General Gates was visiting the congress. "How," Samuel queried, "shall we make him the head of [Schuyler's] army?"

Such conniving did little to endear Adams to the Continental Congress, and even less to endear him to the Continental Army. In the fall of 1777, Adams further damaged his character by being associated with a plot to remove George Washington, the very same general whom John and he had supported to head the American armed forces. The plot arose in September, shortly after Washington's soldiers suffered defeat at Brandywine. A disgruntled army officer named Thomas Conway wrote to congress complaining of Washington's ineffectual leadership, and many delegates began to question the commander's strategy. In October, when news arrived that General Gates had captured Saratoga and forced the surrender of British General John Burgoyne's troops, a few delegates began to lobby discreetly for Gates to replace Washington.

Though Adams's letters are silent on the matter, several of his close allies, James Lovell in particular, were associated with the so-called Conway Cabal. Many spectators believed that Adams also sought Washington's removal, and his political foes were happy to publicize Adams's alleged disloyalty to the commander in chief. As late as 1789, several years after the war's end, Adams still found himself denying the charge of having once opposed the man who now served as the nation's first President.

Nor was Washington the only American leader that Adams managed to offend. Unfortunately, Adams's congressional career was sullied by a series of similar estrangements. Perhaps Adams's most powerful enemy was his former friend, John Hancock. Hancock deeply resented Samuel and John Adams for not nominating him commander in chief. He soon abandoned them both personally and politically, opting instead for the company of the wealthier, more conservative delegates from New York and Virginia. He flaunted his lavish lifestyle, and it was not long before the other Massachusetts representatives came to believe that Hancock was taking advantage of his position as president of the congress. He routinely traveled in an ornate chariot, accompanied by 50 armed horsemen and a slew of servants. He dressed and dined in the most opulent manner and indulged himself in the gaiety of Philadelphia's highest society.

To Samuel and John Adams, Hancock's vanity and luxuriance seemed shamefully inappropriate in a time of war. "Does it become us," Adams asked, "to lead the People to such publick diversions as promote Superfluity of Dress & ornament, when it is as much as they can bear to support the Expense of cloathing a naked Army?" Worse than having offended the Adamses' republican sensibilities, Hancock deeply embarrassed the Massachusetts delegation by holding the presidency even after Peyton Randolph returned from his business in Virginia. So aggrieved was the New England contingent that when Hancock finally did retire from congress, the Adams cousins voted not to thank him for his service as president. They might have chosen their enemies more carefully. For Hancock was still a very powerful man in Massachusetts, and he would not soon forget the Adamses' slights.

Samuel Adams was drawn into another awkward imbroglio through his close relationship with Arthur Lee, the radical Virginian who had long represented American interests in England. After the signing of the Declaration, the congress ordered that Lee travel to Paris, where he would join Benjamin Franklin and Silas Deane as commissioners to France. From the outset, the commissioners' work was hampered by dissension and infighting. This discord resulted from differences in ideology as well as ego—each commissioner had distinct opinions about what sort of man should represent the new nation abroad. But in large part their discord resulted from a lack of clarity about the commissioners' authority. In 1777, the congress recalled Silas Deane, who without congressional permission had offered high-ranking positions in the Continental Army to French noblemen willing to donate money or supplies to the American cause.

Upon returning to Philadelphia, Deane found himself confronting the additional charge of extorting public funds. This accusation was leveled by none other than Arthur Lee's brother, Richard Henry Lee. Intimately associated with the Lee brothers, Samuel Adams soon found himself entangled in the affair. Deane counted Adams among his personal enemies, and he hurried to rally his own supporters in congress to fight in his defense. Aware that Arthur Lee's letters had fueled the congress's investigation into the matter, Deane published an anonymous article in the *Pennsylvania Packet* accusing Lee of traitorously corresponding with a British spy. Adams forwarded several dispatches to his New England associates, assuring them of Lee's innocence. Though Adams wisely chose not to engage in a full-scale newspaper war, the

Deane-Lee affair dragged on for months, and further contributed to his reputation for factiousness.

This reputation, coupled with Adams's lack of expertise in military and diplomatic affairs, contributed to the decline of his prestige in congress after the Declaration of Independence. But if the congress grew disenchanted with Adams, he in turn grew disenchanted with the congress. Nearing his sixtieth year, Adams discovered that his health suffered from the congress's excessive workload. Philadelphia offered "a Climate unfriendly" to his welfare, and to make matters worse, the encroachment of British forces repeatedly necessitated that the delegates flee the city. These hasty travels wore on Adams's aging frame. In February 1778, during a brief respite from congress, Adams at last succumbed to illness; a "bodily disorder" that left him bedridden for "near a fortnight."

But no bodily disorder could compare with the pangs of homesickness Adams felt while he was away from Boston. The busy work of revolution kept Adams in congress often more than a year at a time. He sorely missed "dear Hannah," his beloved daughter who had now grown to adulthood, and Samuel, his "wise Son." And he of course missed his helpmeet, Betsy, who had been forced in her husband's absence to relocate the Adams's household by herself. During the British occupation of Boston, Samuel worried gravely about his wife and her proximity to the fighting. The war made it difficult at times for Betsy to have her letters delivered, and Samuel found himself so busy in Philadelphia that he could not keep regular correspondence. "I can scarsely find time," he once confessed to Betsy, "to write you even a Love Letter." By the end of 1778, Adams was ready to resign from congress and return to his wife and family. To James Warren, Adams confided, "I wish for Retirement & covet Leisure as a Miser does money."

There remained only one final task that Adams wished to see accomplished. In 1776–1777 he had helped to draft the Articles of Confederation, the first charter of govern-

THE DECLARATION OF INDEPENDENCE. JU. 4 1776.

E PLURIBUS UNUM. IN UNITY, THERE IS STRENGTH

ment for the United States. These Articles were hotly contested. Some delegates felt strongly that the confederation
could not survive without a strong national government, a
government that could impose taxes and raise an army for
its defense. Adams, like many others, feared that a powerful
confederation would infringe upon the liberties and auton-
omy of his home state. But Adams was a pragmatist. He
recognized that unless the delegates could agree upon some
form of union, the war with England would likely tear the
states apart. To his friend and ally Richard Henry Lee,
Adams expressed the conviction that "The Confederation,
is most certainly an important Object, and ought to be
attended to & finished speedily."

*This painting conveys
the signing of the
Declaration of Indepen-
dence, with Samuel
Adams seated seventh
from the left, next to
his political ally,
Richard Henry Lee.*

The Articles, however, required certain states to cede control of western lands. For this reason the individual state legislatures were slow to ratify the Articles—the landed states because they did not want to give up their claims in the west, and the "landless" states because they resented such delays. Not until British General Charles Cornwallis began to make inroads toward Virginia did that holdout state finally agree to surrender its land claims. On March 1, 1781, the Articles of Confederation went into effect. A few weeks later, Samuel Adams, who had served in congress now for almost seven full years, finally retired.

The Boston to which Adams returned had changed dramatically from the Boston that he had left behind. The old apparatus of royal government had been dismantled, and after the departure of General Howe, most of Boston's Loyalist citizens fled to more hospitable climes. While the war continued in other parts of the country, the people of Massachusetts were left to reclaim their lives and homes and businesses, and to rebuild their fortunes after the ravaging effects of the blockade. Adams's own home was made unlivable during the occupation and he and his family now took up residence in a house that had been confiscated from a Tory named Robert Hallowell.

Soon, however, the Hallowell house lost a resident, for just after Adams arrived back in Boston, his daughter married a young Bostonian named Thomas Wells. During the previous winter, Wells had asked Samuel Adams for Hannah's hand in marriage. Adams happily consented, and offered Wells some fatherly advice. He urged the young bridegroom "not to govern too much," and he emphasized the importance of piety. "Religion in a Family," Adams wrote his future son-in-law, "is at once its brightest Ornament & its best Security."

Adams's political life was changing too. He had been gone from Massachusetts for several years. In his absence, John Hancock strove to displace him as the first man in Massachusetts politics. Adams nevertheless managed to stay

THE MARRIAGE STATE

While Samuel Adams was away at the Continental Congress, his daughter Hannah became engaged to marry a young man named Thomas Wells. In November 1780, Adams wrote Wells to welcome him into the family and to offer his advice on marriage. His letter reflects the notion at the time that a man ought to be the head of his household, but it also reflects Adams's concern for his daughter's happiness, his unique religious sensibility, and his own desire to return home.

My Dear Mr Wells   Philadelphia Novr 22 1780

The Marriage State was designd to complete the Sum of human Happiness in this Life. It some times proves otherwise; but this is owing to the Parties themselves, who either rush into it without due Consideration, or fail in point of Discretion in the Conduct towards each other .... When the married Couple strictly observe the great Rules of Honor & Justice towards each other, Differences, if any happen, between them, must proceed from small & trifling Circumstances. Of what Consequence is it, whether a Turkey is brought on the Table boild or roasted? And yet, how often are the Passions sufferd to interfere in such mighty Disputes, till the tempers of both become so sowerd, that they can scarcely look upon each other with any tolerable Degree of good Humor.... I feel myself at this Moment so domestically disposd that I could say a thousand things to you, if I had Leisure. I could dwell on the Importance of Piety & Religion, of Industry & Frugality, of Prudence, Economy, Regularity & an even Government, all which are essential to the Well being of a Family. But I have not Time. I cannot however help repeating Piety, because I think it indispensible. Religion in a Family is at once its brightest Ornament & its best Security... Nothing certainly being so great a Debt upon us, as to render to the Creator & Preserver those Acknowledgments which are due to Him for our Being, and the hourly Protection he affords us.

       Remember me to all Friends, and be assured that I am

                                Yours

active in the affairs of his home state. While he attended the Continental Congress, Adams's friends in Boston kept him apprised of local developments, and he was repeatedly elected to public office, despite Hancock's efforts. He of course held a seat in the House of Representatives, he was elected a member of the Massachusetts Council, and he served as secretary of state, all during his tenure in Philadelphia.

In 1779, Samuel Adams and his cousin John both attended the state's constitutional convention, and they along with James Bowdoin were selected by the convention to write a new constitution. One year earlier, Massachusetts had tried and failed to frame a constitution to replace its ramshackle provisional government, which had been operating since 1775. John Adams, Massachusetts' foremost legal and constitutional thinker, took the lead in writing the draft, but Samuel was chosen to write Article III of the Declaration of the Rights of the Inhabitants of the Commonwealth of Massachusetts, which addressed the subject of religion.

That Samuel Adams undertook this project is hardly surprising; his faith had always been strong, and it became more prominent in his writings and thoughts as he grew older. In fact, Adams's vision for the new commonwealth reflected a blend of religious values and republican ideals. He looked both to the charity and humility of his Puritan ancestors and to the austerity and discipline of the Greek nation-states. One day, Adams hoped, Massachusetts would become a "Christian Sparta," exemplifying the best of both of those models.

While Adams looked to the past, however, many New Englanders looked to the future, and some objected to Adams's contributions to the new constitution. Most problematic was the provision of Article III that required all citizens of Massachusetts to pay taxes to their church. Individuals who did not belong to a congregation were required to pay into the Congregational Church. Additionally, Article III imposed legal barriers to the recognition of new sects. In Boston alone, these provisions generated protest from more than 400 voters. Nevertheless, the town meetings of Massachusetts ratified the constitution, and Article III remained on the books for four decades.

In furtherance of his vision for Massachusetts, Adams also co-founded the Academy of Arts and Sciences in 1780. Like many scientific and philosophic organizations of its day, the Academy was designed to promote the knowledge necessary for an informed and conscientious public. To Adams's dismay, however, the people of Massachusetts seemed uninterested in such noble pursuits. All around him he saw extravagance and prodigality. The new government, he lamented, exhibited "more Pomp & Parade than is consistent with those sober Republican Principles" upon which it was founded. To Adams, history had demonstrated that luxury would make a citizenry soft and complacent. John Winthrop and the Puritan settlers, Adams believed, "would have revolted" at the "Scenes of Dissipation & Folly" that he now saw in Massachusetts. Much of this he blamed on men such as the newly elected governor, John Hancock, whose ostentation set a standard that the people were eager to follow.

In 1784, Adams was grieved to witness the formation in Boston of a new organization known as the Sans Souci Club. The members of this club, whose name was French for "Without a Care," were drawn from the highest ranks of Boston society. They sponsored balls, teas, and other sorts of social events that Adams believed would corrupt a virtuous people. "You would be surprized," Samuel wrote his cousin, John, "to see the Equipage, the Furniture, and expensive Living of too many, the Pride and Vanity of Dress which pervades thro every class." Adams also spoke out against the Order of Cincinnati, a society of Revolutionary War officers that met to deliberate political matters, because he feared that the veterans would form themselves into the same sort of hereditary aristocracy that had spoiled England.

For years Adams continued to fight against the degradation of public morals. In 1790 he led a protest against the

establishment of theaters in Boston. Since the reign of
Queen Elizabeth, religious reformers such as the Puritans
had fought against theaters because plays were thought to
be sinful. Public performances distracted audiences from
their Christian responsibilities, and the theaters themselves
were filled with scandal and vice. Actors, whose profession
required that they pretend to be people they were not, were
distrusted and shunned.

To his friend John Scollay, Adams professed, "I love the
People of Boston." Yet he had come to despair his neighbors' lack of virtue. "I once thought that City would be the
Christian Sparta. But Alass! Will men never be free! They
will be free no longer than while they remain virtuous."
But Adams could not keep the theaters out of Boston any
more than he could he stem the people's longing for enter-
tainment, wealth, and opulence. His old ally James Warren
complained that Adams had become "the most arbitrary
and despotic Man in the Commonwealth."

Neither Adams's disappointment about the decline of
public virtue nor the enmity of former friends could keep
him out of office. In 1783, Adams lost an election for lieutenant governor to Thomas Cushing, the moderate Whig
with whom he had served in the Continental Congress
years before. But that same year, Adams was reelected to the
Massachusetts Senate and once again chosen to serve as its
president. It was while holding this high office that Adams
received news of the Treaty of Paris, which formally
brought an end to the Revolution, and by which the
United States was officially recognized as a sovereign nation.
It must have been an extremely gratifying occasion for
Adams, who had done so much to bring about the rebellion, to see America finally emerge victorious.

But while others celebrated, Adams urged caution. To
Richard Henry Lee, Adams wrote, "By Gods Blessing on
the Councils & the Arms of our Country, we are now rank'd
with Nations. May He keep us from exulting beyond Measure!

No Christian Sparta

Samuel Adams was disappointed that the Massachusetts Constitution, which he helped to write, was unable to instill virtue in the citizenry of his common-wealth. In this letter to his friend, John Scollay, Adams rails against the new government, and the extravagance and luxury that had captivated the people.

My dear Sir   Philade Decr 30 1780

Our Government, I perceive, is organizd on the Basis of the new Constitution. I am affraid there is more Pomp & Parade than is consis-tent with those sober Republican Principles, upon which the Framers of it thought they had founded it. Why should this new Era be intro-ducd with Entertainments expensive & tending to dissipate the Minds of the People? Does it become us to lead the People to such publick diversions as promote Superfluity of Dress & ornament, when it is as much as they can bear to support the Expense of cloathing a naked Army? Will Vanity & Levity ever be the Stability of government, either in States, in Cities, or what, let me hint to you is of the last Importance, in Families? Of what Kind are those Manners, by which, as we are truly informd in a late Speech, "not only the freedom but the very Existence of Republicks is greatly affected?" How fruitless is it, to recommend "the adapting the Laws in the most perfect Manner possi-ble, to the Suppression of Idleness, Dissipation & Extravagancy, " if such Recommendations are counteracted by the Example of Men of Religion, Influence & publick Station?...But I fear I shall say too much. I love the People of Boston. I once thought, that City would be the Christian Sparta. But Alass! Will men never be free! They will be free no longer than while they remain virtuous. Sidney tells us, there are times when People are not worth saving. Meaning, when they have lost their Virtue. I pray God, this may never be truly said of my beloved Town. Adieu.

Great Pains are yet to be taken & much Wisdom is requisite that we may stand as a Nation in a respectable Character."

Adams's warnings were perhaps well founded, for as the early years of American nationhood attested, the country's leaders had not yet hammered out solutions to all of the United States' social and political ills. Never was this more evident than in western Massachusetts during the summer of 1786. Farmers in that part of the state were struggling for financial survival. Their crisis arose because the Massachusetts legislature had imposed a series of high taxes in order to repay the state's enormous war debt. Exacerbating the farmers' money problems was the fact that New England merchants had successfully lobbied against paper money. Western Massachusetts farmers, unfortunately, had little specie with which to repay their debts, and local creditors began to foreclose upon their property.

Threatened with bankruptcy and the loss of their family farms, many rural citizens rallied around a Revolutionary War veteran named Captain Daniel Shays. Shays and his followers marched on local courts and, under threat of force, prohibited the county judges from foreclosing on their property. Shays' Rebellion, as the movement came to be known, rapidly expanded. Some 1,100 farmers joined in the uprising, and even threatened to seize a federal arsenal. Once armed with such weapons, the Shaysites intended to take control of the countryside until the legislature granted them financial relief.

The irony of the rebellion lay in the fact that Shays and his men were fighting against taxation, much as Samuel Adams and his Patriot allies had done years before. Fisher Ames, a conservative Massachusetts statesmen, observed, "The people have turned against their teachers the doctrines which were inculcated to effect the late revolution." Samuel Adams had little patience with such arguments. This was not a case of taxation without representation. Unlike the colonists, who had no access to Parliament, the farmers of western Massachusetts could demand that their elected representatives repeal the injurious legislation, or they could vote those representatives out of office.

With such legal recourse at hand, there seemed to Adams no justification for violent resistance. And with the welfare of the state, and indeed of the entire union, at stake, Adams believed that the taking up of arms by the Shaysites amounted to the highest treason. Adams encouraged Governor Bowdoin to suppress the rebellion, calling upon national troops if necessary. For the leaders of the insurgency, Adams proposed nothing short of execution. "The man who dares to rebel against the laws of a republic," Adams proclaimed, "ought to suffer death." Fortunately for Shays' followers, the governor saw fit to pardon them from that severe penalty.

Shays' Rebellion was only one of many debtor uprisings in New England. Similar insurrections broke out in Vermont, Connecticut, and New Hampshire, in the middle states of New York and Pennsylvania, and as far south as Virginia and the Carolinas, causing many prominent American politicians to fear for the security of the union. Most American leaders already believed that the Articles of Confederation, which granted the Congress no power to levy taxes or raise an army, were too weak to hold the states together. Collectively, these anxieties spurred the growth of a national constitutional reform movement. In Mount Vernon, Virginia, in 1785, and in Annapolis, Maryland, in 1786, advocates of constitutional reform helped to set the agenda of American politics. The Annapolis gathering recommended that a new convention be organized for the specific purpose of revising the Articles, and the Confederation Congress agreed.

In May 1787, the Constitutional Convention met in Philadelphia. Those in attendance deliberated such issues as the number of representatives each state would send to the national legislature, the future of slavery, and the ability of

The debate over the Constitution spawned rancorous arguments between those who supported ratification and those who supported it. In this engraving, the state of Connecticut is represented as a wagon overburdened with wartime debt. Federalist and Anti-Federalist supporters trade vulgar insults.

the national congress to impose a tax for the purpose of raising revenue. After four arduous months of debate and compromise, the delegates signed their names to the United States Constitution. All that remained for it to become law was ratification by nine of the thirteen states.

Samuel Adams was not elected to attend the Constitutional Convention, but he was chosen to serve at the Massachusetts ratifying convention. When he first learned about the proposed Constitution, Adams was skeptical. As far south as Virginia, James Madison heard rumors that Adams objected to the Constitution because it contained no religious qualification for candidates for public office. But this was not Adams's objection. Adams, rather, believed that the proposed Constitution surrendered too much power to the national government. Like many Americans who found themselves saddled with the name Anti-Federalists, Adams feared that the individual states would lose authority over their internal affairs. As he explained to Richard Henry Lee, "If the several States in the Union are to become one entire Nation, under one Legislature, the Powers of which shall extend to every Subject of Legislation, and its Laws be supreme & controul the whole, the Idea of Sovereignty in the States must be lost."

Adams also worried that the proposed legislative branch would not be able to accommodate the "local Habits, Feelings, Views & Interests" of citizens living in the various states. "Is it to be expected," Adams rhetorically asked, "that General Laws can be adapted to the Feelings of the more Eastern and the more Southern Parts of so extensive a Nation?" Foremost among Adams's concerns must have been the issue of slavery. In the Constitutional Convention, the debates over that "peculiar institution" had revealed strong regional divisions, divisions that would erupt into civil war several decades later. Adams may have worried about the fitness of a union in which some people opposed slavery while others were heavily invested in it.

Adams was well aware, though, that many New Englanders did not share his anxieties about the proposed Constitution. Federalists, who supported the Constitution, prevailed in coastal cities such as Boston, where merchants and tradesmen demanded a stronger, centralized government to regulate trade with England and the rest of Europe. A younger generation of politicians, spearheaded by Federalists such as Fisher Ames, persuaded many citizens that the future of Massachusetts depended on a formidable national union.

At the ratifying convention, most of the opposition to the new Constitution came from western Massachusetts, but these rural delegates were less organized and less experienced in political affairs than their Federalist counterparts. They also bore the taint of having been associated with the lawlessness of Shays' Rebellion. The Federalists, in contrast, were a cohesive faction that counted among their ranks several of Massachusetts' leading men. More importantly, the Federalists employed shrewd political strategy to secure ratification. In January 1788, the Federalists approached Paul Revere and urged him to use his influence to win Adams over to the cause of the new Constitution.

For Adams, one curious consequence of his opposition to the Constitution was an unexpected reconciliation with his rival, Governor John Hancock. Both feared that the new government would encroach upon the state powers of Massachusetts. However, both realized that the United States might not survive without stronger government, and men such as Paul Revere, men they had long trusted, supported the new charter. The two aging statesmen were also reunited by personal tragedies. Both had recently lost their only sons. In January 1787, Hancock's nine-year-old son, John George Washington Hancock, died of injuries sustained during an ice-skating accident. One year later, Samuel Adams Jr., whose health had suffered since his days working as an army doctor, died of tuberculosis. The sorrow-stricken fathers recognized that they had more in common now than perhaps ever before and they tentatively began working together again.

Perhaps reminded of their glory days, Adams and Hancock devised a plan that would unite moderates in both the Federalist and Anti-Federalist camps, forming a narrow majority in support of the Constitution. The plan, which Governor Hancock presented to the ratifying convention in a dramatic personal appearance, consisted of a list of recommended amendments. These provisions would not be prerequisite conditions for Massachusetts to agree to the Constitution, as some Anti-Federalists had demanded, but they would help to set the agenda of the first federal Congress to meet under the Constitution. On February 6, 1788, by a vote of 189 to 168, the convention approved the plan and endorsed the Constitution and the recommended amendments. Several states followed Massachusetts' lead by ratifying the Constitution and proposing their own amendments. Three years later, the amendments proposed by the various states were trimmed down, redrafted, and adopted by Congress as the Bill of Rights.

During the debate over national government, Adams had not lost sight of local matters, and he had come to understand that the political sands were shifting beneath his feet. In 1788, he lost a highly contested bid for the U.S. House of Representatives to the up-and-coming Federalist candidate, Fisher Ames. After this defeat, Adams recognized that in order to remain active in Massachusetts affairs, he would need to take advantage of what few alliances had survived decades of political and personal tumult. In 1789, when John Hancock once again ran for the governor's seat, Adams agreed to run as his lieutenant. After 15 years of bitter political quarrels, the recently reconciled Patriots were elected on the same ticket.

Adams was now an old man. He had witnessed his daughter, Hannah, grow to adulthood and start her own family. And he had witnessed his son, Samuel, die at the young age of 37 from an extended illness. Adams and his wife, Betsy, moved from their temporary home in the Hallowell House to a more suitable abode on Winter Street. A stone's throw from the Common, this three-story house formerly belonged to a Tory named Sylvanus Gardiner, who abandoned it during the war. It was painted yellow, and had a small courtyard and a garden. There the Adamses made due on Samuel's modest salary and on their son's army pension. Samuel Adams invested this money in real estate in the neighboring town of Jamaica Plain. Adams's first successful business venture, this investment sustained the couple for the rest of their lives.

Adams served as Hancock's lieutenant for four years, and upon Hancock's death in 1793, he ascended to the governor's chair. By that time, political life in the United States had begun to stabilize. But in Europe there raged a tempest. The French Revolution was well under way, and the spirit of *égalité* promised to destroy that nation's oldest institutions. Unlike many American leaders, who were horrified by the violent excesses of the so-called "Reign of Terror," Adams respected the democratic spirit of the French people. Their thirst for liberty and their selfless commitment to the eradication of hierarchy inspired him. Most of all, Adams admired the French because they endeavored to establish a republic, the form of government that he believed was most fit to protect the rights and property of the people.

Adams was not so enamored with the administration of his own country. In January 1789, a group of Presidential electors, authorized by the Confederation Congress and selected by the individual states, unanimously elected George Washington the first President of the United States. Since that time, the Federalist Party had continued to grow, especially in Massachusetts. The national government also continued to expand, and with it swelled an enormous public debt.

President Washington's secretary of the treasury, an ambitious New York lawyer named Alexander Hamilton, developed a fiscal policy that, in Adams's view, favored bankers and merchants over farmers and workingmen. In 1790, Hamilton convinced the President to charter a new Bank of the United States. Hamilton's opponents, Thomas Jefferson most prominent among them, had grave misgivings about consolidating so much of the nation's economic power into a single financial institution. Jefferson's adherents also argued for a narrow construction of the Constitution; nowhere did that document explicitly authorize the federal government to charter a bank.

More offensive to Adams than the Federalist economic platform was the Federalist political sensibility. Most Federalist proponents favored a more powerful national government. They typically envisioned an America presided over by elite statesmen: merchants, lawyers, and planters who had risen to the highest political and social rank. To be sure, the Federalists agreed with the Whig belief that political power derived from the people. But more so than the followers of Jefferson, the Federalists thought the people would be better served if that power were entrusted to patrician leaders.

The problem with such a system, Adams believed, was that ordinary citizens would soon lose their voice in government. When John Adams, who strongly supported the Federalist cause, argued that in a republic "the People have an essential *share* in the sovereignty," his more democratic cousin gently corrected him: "Is not the *whole* sovereignty, my friend, essentially in the People?"

As a republican-minded governor in a Federalist state, however, there was little Adams could do to suppress the Federalist impulse. Through most of Washington's Presidency, Federalism prevailed as the dominant ideology in U. S. politics. Not until the struggle over the Bank of the United States did the Democratic-Republican Party begin to coalesce. In 1796, that party nominated Thomas Jefferson to run as Washington's successor. The Federalists countered by nominating John Adams. Notwithstanding their bond of kinship and the many years that they had collaborated against the British administration, Samuel did not support his cousin's bid for the Presidency. To the contrary, Adams held such firm convictions against the Federalist agenda that he ran in Massachusetts as a Presidential elector in support of Thomas Jefferson. He was soundly defeated.

Sensing that his political days had come to an end, Samuel Adams announced his retirement from politics shortly thereafter. On January 27, 1797, Adams stood before the Massachusetts legislature and announced that he would not seek reelection to the governor's office. "The infirmities of age," Adams announced, "render me an unfit person in my own opinion, and probably in the opinion of others, to continue in this station." At 75 years of age, after 40 exhausting years of public service, Adams at last stepped down.

Adams, of course, remained in Boston after his retirement. He loved to spend time with his family, especially his three grandchildren, and with old friends who enjoyed reminiscing about how much the world had changed. Over time, though, Adams's health deteriorated and his infirmities became apparent. While still in office, Adams had fallen after delivering a speech before the legislature, and during Hancock's funeral, Adams had not been able to walk with the procession. Now his palsy worsened such that he could no longer write without the assistance of a secretary.

Yet his mind remained sound, and his political passions as fierce as ever. In 1800, Adams rejoiced to see Thomas Jefferson elected President of the United States. Adams took great comfort in the so-called "revolution of 1800." To Adams, Jefferson's election represented a triumph not only for the Democratic-Republicans, but for the very principles for which the American Revolution had been fought. Writing to congratulate his old friend from Virginia, Adams declared, "The Storm is now over, and we are in port."

Adams's final letter, though, was written in 1802 to Thomas Paine, the author of the incendiary tract, *Common Sense,* who later journeyed to Europe in support of the French Revolution. Adams first thanked Paine for his pamphlets, which "unquestionably awakened the public mind, and led the people loudly to call for a declaration of our national independence." But Adams had heard a disquieting rumor that Paine was now writing an attack on Christianity. In *The Age of Reason,* Paine proclaimed his belief in one God who created the universe, but he rejected with scorn the belief that the Bible was divinely inspired.

The doctrine of divine inspiration, Paine argued, was invented by priests to cement their power over ordinary men and women. Not persuaded by Paine's arguments, Adams held firm to his Christian faith. He was appalled by Paine's attack on the revealed wisdom of the Old and New Testaments, and he scolded the pamphleteer for striving to "unchristianize the mass of our citizens." But more than wanting to reform Paine's religious convictions, Adams worried that Paine's pamphlet, if widely circulated in the United States, would create such a controversy that some people might argue against the freedom of the press.

"Neither religion nor liberty," Adams warned Paine, "can long subsist in the tumult of altercation and amidst the noise and violence of faction."

How fitting it was that after years of struggle Adams spent his final days fighting for religion and liberty. In the months that followed his letter to Paine, Adams grew increasingly ill. In autumn he became bedridden, and on October 3, 1803, Adams died in the presence of his wife and several family friends.

EPILOGUE: SAMUEL ADAMS'S LEGACY

News of Adams's death spread quickly through Boston, and the town's church bells began to toll in his memory. His funeral was scheduled for Thursday, October 7, but at the time of Adams's death, Governor Caleb Strong was away from Boston on business. Lieutenant Governor Robbins had no legal power to order the sort of military procession that usually attended the funerals of great statesmen. So Adams's friends and family instead planned a plain procession, of which Adams would have greatly approved, consisting only of his widow and "two '75 men, who had never forsaken their old principles." But Lieutenant Governor Robbins got word of this plan, and began to worry what the people of Boston might think about his refusal to honor the great patriot. Acting without authority, Robbins ordered a full funeral parade. Robbins himself agreed to serve as a pallbearer.

At four o'clock in the afternoon, Adams's casket was marched through the streets of Boston behind a military escort and a corps of cadets. Behind the casket walked Adams's widow, Betsy, and daughter, Hannah, with her husband and children. Following Adams's family, a train of federal and state officials, Harvard faculty, local clergy, foreign consuls, members of the Academy of Arts and Sciences and the Massachusetts Charitable Society, militia officers, and private citizens filed by. This grand cortege traveled along Washington Street, where shopkeepers had closed their businesses. Cannons fired on every minute, and in the harbor, ships flew their flags at half-mast. After passing the state house, the procession marched on to the Old Granary burial ground, where Adams was laid in his family tomb.

A couple of weeks later, Adams's death was announced before the U.S. House of Representatives. After a brief eulogy, the House unanimously resolved that it was "penetrated with a full sense of the eminent services rendered to his country in the most arduous times by the late Samuel Adams." The members further resolved to wear "crape on the left arm for one month in testimony of the national gratitude and reverence towards the memory of that undaunted and illustrious patriot." The following January, when the Massachusetts General Court again convened, its members voted to wear black, but, ironically, with much less unanimity. The Massachusetts House was fraught with political animosities. Though the Federalists begrudgingly agreed to acknowledge the accomplishment of their old adversary, they would not acquiesce to great fanfare.

Perhaps it was natural for the Massachusetts lawmakers to resist memorializing Adams. He had not held office for many years, and his service as governor had been lackluster. More significantly, three full decades had passed since Adams's Sons of Liberty ruled the town. Adams had long outlived many of his fellow Patriots, and a new generation of politicians had

In 1754, Benjamin Franklin published this political cartoon: a snake cut into segments, representing the colonies on the eve of the French and Indian War, with the motto "Join or Die." Twenty years later, shortly after news of the Boston Port Bill reached the colonies, Paul Revere modified the design, again to urge colonial unity.

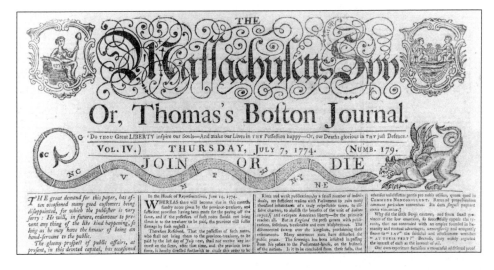

arisen. This was a generation that barely remembered the night when the Liberty Boys tore down Andrew Oliver's stamp office. The politicians of 1803 had not seen the blood on King Street, and they had only heard stories of the destruction of the tea. Who was Samuel Adams, to them, but an old relic, out of touch with time and the people?

But during the fight for American independence, Adams had been much more. More than any other single individual, Adams was responsible for making the Revolution happen. He kept the people of Massachusetts vigilant in defense of their liberties. He drew attention to acts of tyranny that others were prepared to tolerate. He reached out to the other colonies and found like-minded Patriots who would support the cause. He continued to test the patience of the royal government until, at long last, Parliament issued the Coercive Acts. And he urged the citizens of Massachusetts to arm themselves, forcing General Gage to march on Concord. It was these events that shaped public sentiment and that ultimately led to the Declaration of Independence.

To be sure, Adams did not act alone. Much radical leadership came from the firebrand colony of Virginia, and even in Massachusetts, Adams depended on men such as James Otis, John Hancock, John Adams, and Paul Revere. But it was Adams who kept the resistance movement alive and Adams who took the lead in pre-Revolutionary politics. In 1775, a British officer wrote back to England, "Would you believe it that this immense continent, from New England to Georgia, is moved and directed by one man!-a man of ordinary birth and desperate fortune, who, by his abilities and talent for factious intrigue, has made himself of some consequence . . . . This is the case of our great patriot and leader, Sam Adams." John Adams declared that his cousin had been "born and tempered a wedge of steel to split the knot of *lignum vitae* [lifeline], which tied North America to Great Britain."

After his death, one Boston newspaper even proclaimed Adams the "Father of the American Revolution."

Samuel Adams, however, never thought of himself in such terms. "It is often stated that I am at the head of the Revolution." Rather, Adams explained, "a few of us merely lead the way as the people follow, and we can go no further than we are backed up by them; for if we attempt to advance any further, we make no progress and may lose our labor in defeat." This was a lesson Adams had learned by experience. In the periods of calm after the repeal of the Stamp Act and again after the massacre trials, Adams found himself almost completely abandoned by the popular party. Later during the campaign for the Declaration of Independence, Adams was forced to restrain his natural impulses, conscious of the fact that if he pushed too far ahead, most Americans would not follow.

For Adams, then, the Revolution belonged to the people. Throughout his political career, Adams's foremost objective was to secure for the citizens of Massachusetts the right to govern themselves. In pursuit of his goal, Adams made the most of his strengths: a golden pen, a shrewd sense of political strategy, and a keen ability to rally individuals in support of a common cause. He was motivated in part by personal politics, in particular by having watched his father, Deacon Adams, suffer at the hands of the court party. But he was also motivated by a profound faith in the common man. From his readings of Locke and other Whig thinkers Adams came to understand that the power to rule derived from the people. He believed that once sovereignty was secured in a republican government, virtuous, well-educated citizens would always keep their leaders in check. Adams once wrote, "The Love of Liberty is interwoven in the Soul of Man." By fighting for independence, Adams gave back to the citizens of America the liberty that had been usurped by a tyrannical king and a corrupt Parliament. Liberty was Adams's passion, and liberty is his legacy.

CHRONOLOGY

September 22, 1722
Samuel Adams is born in Boston, Massachusetts

1736–40
Adams attends Harvard College, where he is ranked sixth in his class

1743
Adams earns his master's degree from Harvard College

1747
Deacon Adams is nominated to serve on the governor's council, but Governor Shirley vetoes the nomination; Samuel Adams forms a political club with several friends, and they soon begin to publish the *Independent Advertiser*

March 1748
Deacon Adams dies at the age of 59

October 17, 1749
Adams and Elizabeth Checkley are married

1750–53
Elizabeth Adams bears four children; only a son, Samuel, survives infancy

July 1756
Samuel and Elizabeth Adams have another girl, named Hannah

July 1758
Elizabeth Adams delivers a stillborn child, and dies soon thereafter; Adams successfully fights an effort to foreclose on his family property, which results from his father's land bank debts

1753–65
Adams serves in a series of minor local offices, including scavenger, chimney inspector, school inspector, and tax collector

1764
Adams instructs Boston's representatives in the General Court to oppose the Sugar Act

December 6, 1764
Adams marries Elizabeth Wells

August 1765
The Sons of Liberty riot against the Stamp Act

September 27, 1765
Adams is sworn in as a member of the General Court of Massachusetts; soon thereafter he authors the Massachusetts Resolves

May 1766
Adams is elected clerk of the General Court

October 1767
Adams first proposes nonimportation

1770–71
Adams writes in the local papers as "A Chatterer," "Vindex," and "Candidus"

March 5, 1770
Several members of the 29th regiment open fire on Boston citizens; five are killed and several more injured in what soon becomes known as the Boston Massacre

1771
Adams loses an election for the position of Registrar of Deeds to a Tory opponent

October 1772
Writing in the local paper as "Valerius Poplicola," Adams attempts to provoke public outcry over the issue of governors' and judges' salaries, which are now to be paid by the king, rather than by the people of Massachusetts

November 1772
Adams organizes committees of correspondence; Adams authors "The Rights of the Colonists"

June 1773
Adams publishes Governor Hutchinson's private letters, destroying his reputation

December 16, 1773
The Sons of Liberty dump 342 chests of tea into Boston Harbor

June 1774
The House of Representatives nominates Adams and others to attend the Continental Congress

September–October, 1774
The First Continental Congress convenes, adopts the Suffolk Resolves, ratifies a Declaration of Rights, and appeals to King George III for redress

April 19, 1775
The Battles of Lexington and Concord are fought

May 1775
Adams attends the Second Continental Congress, which meets more or less continuously throughout the Revolution; during his absence from Massachusetts, Adams is elected to the House of Representatives and the governor's council, and he is elected secretary of state

June 1775
John and Samuel Adams support George Washington, rather than John Hancock, as commander in chief; Hancock and

Adams once again become enemies; Dr. Joseph Warren is killed at the Battle of Bunker Hill

January 1776
Thomas Paine's *Common Sense* is published, convincing many Americans of the need for independence

July 4, 1776
The Second Continental Congress approves the Declaration of Independence

March 1778
The Articles of Confederation go into effect, and shortly thereafter Adams retires from congress

1779
Adams authors that portion of the Massachusetts Constitution dealing with religion

1780
Adams co-founds the Academy of Arts and Sciences

1781
Adams is elected to the Massachusetts Senate, and is chosen its president

1783
Adams loses his bid for lieutenant governor, but is re-elected to the Massachusetts Senate; the Treaty of Paris is signed, bringing a formal conclusion to the Revolutionary War

1786
Adams advises Governor Bowdoin to execute the leaders of Shays' Rebellion

1788
Paul Revere convinces Adams to support the United States Constitution, which is subsequently ratified in June; Adams loses a subsequent election for the U.S. House of Representatives to Federalist candidate, Fisher Ames

1789
Hancock and Adams are reconciled, and are elected governor and lieutenant governor, respectively, of Massachusetts

1793
Upon Hancock's death, Adams ascends to the governor's seat

1794
Adams is elected governor

1796
For the U.S. Presidency, Adams campaigns for Democratic-Republican nominee Thomas Jefferson, rather than for his Federalist cousin, John Adams

October 3, 1803
Adams dies in his Boston home

FURTHER READING

WRITING BY SAMUEL ADAMS

Cushing, Harry Alonzo, ed. *The Writings of Samuel Adams*. 4 vols. New York: Octagon Books, 1968.

BIOGRAPHIES OF SAMUEL ADAMS

Alexander, John K. *Samuel Adams: America's Revolutionary Politician*. Lanham, Md: Rowman & Littlefield, 2002.

Fowler, William M., Jr. *Samuel Adams: Radical Puritan*. New York: Longman, 1997.

Fradin, Dennis B. *Samuel Adams: the Father of American Independence*. New York: Clarion, 1998.

Galvin, John R. *Three Men of Boston*. New York: Thomas Y. Crowell, 1976.

Hosmer, James Kendall. *Samuel Adams*. New York: AMS Press, 1972.

Maier, Pauline. *The Old Revolutionaries: Political Lives in the Age of Samuel Adams*. New York: Knopf, 1980.

Wells, William V. *The Life and Public Services of Samuel Adams*. 3 vols. Boston: Little, Brown, 1865.

BIOGRAPHIES OF PROMINENT FIGURES DURING THE AMERICAN REVOLUTION

Akers, Charles W. *Abigail Adams, An American Woman*. Boston: Little, Brown, 1980.

Ayer, A. J. *Thomas Paine*. New York: Atheneum, 1988.

Bailyn, Bernard. *The Ordeal of Thomas Hutchinson*. Cambridge: Harvard University Press, 1974.

Cunningham, Noble E. *In Pursuit of Reason: The Life of Thomas Jefferson*. New York: Ballantine, 1988.

Ellis, Joseph J. *Passionate Sage: The Character and Legacy of John Adams*. New York: W.W. Norton, 1993.

Ferling, John E. *John Adams: A Bibliography*. Knoxville: University of Tennessee Press, 1992.

Fischer, David Hackett. *Paul Revere's Ride*. New York: Oxford University Press, 1994.

Fowler, William M., Jr. *The Baron of Beacon Hill: A Biography of John Hancock*. Boston: Houghton Mifflin, 1980.

Keller, Rosemary Skinner. *Abigail Adams and the American Revolution: A Personal History*. New York: Arno Press, 1982.

Koslow, Philip. *John Hancock: A Signature Life*. New York: Franklin Watts, 1998.

Middlekauff, Robert. *Benjamin Franklin and His Enemies*. Berkeley: University of California Press, 1996.

Pencak, William. *America's Burke: The Mind of Thomas Hutchinson*. Washington, D.C.: University Press of America, 1982.

Philp, Mark. *Paine*. New York: Oxford University Press, 1989.

Skemp, Sheila L. *Benjamin and William Franklin: Father and Son, Patriot and Loyalist*. Boston: Bedford, 1994.

Triber, Jayne E. *A True Republican: The Life of Paul Revere*. Amherst: University of Massachusetts Press, 1998.

Wright, Esmond. *Franklin of Philadelphia*. Cambridge: Harvard University Press, 1986.

Boston During the American Revolution

Birnbaum, Louis. *Red Dawn at Lexington*. Boston: Houghton Mifflin, 1986.

Lucier, Armand Francis, ed. *Journal of Occurrences: Patriot Propaganda on the British Occupation Of Boston, 1768–1769*. Bowie, Md.: Heritage Books, 1996.

Pencak, William. *War, Politics, and Revolution in Provincial Massachusetts*. Boston: Northeastern University Press, 1981.

Young, Alfred Fabian. *The Shoemaker and the Tea Party: Memory and the American Revolution*. Boston: Beacon Press, 1999.

Zobel, Hiller B. *The Boston Massacre*. New York: W.W. Norton, 1970.

INDEX

Picture Credits

American Antiquarian Society: 8, 18–19, 43, 54, 57; Boston Athenaeum: 74; Bostonian Society: 50; Colonial Williamsburg Foundation: 120, 136, 145; Gilder Lehrman Collection: 118; Library of Congress: frontispiece, 62, 88, 105, 109, 123, 138, 154; Massachusetts Historical Society: 29, 34, 43; Museum of Fine Arts, Boston: cover, 97; National Archives: 110, 114, 131; New York Public Library: 9, 13, 23, 31, 39, 83, 127; Scottish National Portrait Gallery: 69.

Text Credits

Citizens and Soldiers, p. 78: Samuel Adams to the *Boston Gazette,* December 12, 1768.

In a Gore of Blood, p. 85: Elizabeth Cuming to an unknown recipient, October 28, 1769, James Murray Robbins Family Papers, Massachusetts Historical Society.

The Rights of the Colonists, p. 98: Henry Alonzo Cushing, ed., *The Writings of Samuel Adams* (New York: Octagon Books, 1968), 350–69.

An Easy, Genteel Figure, p. 132: Paul H. Smith, ed., *Letters of Delegates to Congress, 1774–1789* (Washington, D.C.: Library of Congress, 1976–2000), 24–25.

The Marriage State, p. 147: Henry Alonzo Cushing, ed., *The Writings of Samuel Adams* (New York: Octagon Books, 1968), 223–24.

No Christian Sparta, p. 151: Henry Alonzo Cushing, ed., *The Writings of Samuel Adams* (New York: Octagon Books, 1968), 236–39.

ACKNOWLEDGMENTS

As ever, my foremost debt of gratitude belongs to Jane Kamensky, a remarkable mentor who recommended me to Oxford University Press and who continues to teach me, both by example and by instruction, what it is to write a book. At every step, I aspire to her standard. I am also deeply obliged to David Hackett Fischer, who first encouraged me to research pre-Revolutionary Boston and whose own narrative of Paul Revere's ride, a model of thoughtful history and elegant writing, has been a great inspiration for this biography.

Richard B. Bernstein brought his masterly command of both history and historiography to bear on the first draft of the manuscript. I am thankful for the embarrassment he spared me; more thankful for the friendship he did not. Another esteemed colleague, Jenny Hale Pulsipher, lent her expertise on Metacom's War with characteristic kindness and support.

I am very appreciative of the librarians and staffs of the New York Public Library, the American Antiquarian Society, the Massachusetts Historical Society, and the David Library of the American Revolution for providing gracious assistance despite my supreme ineptitude handling rare books and microfilm.

At Oxford, I would like to thank my editor, Nancy Toff, for proposing Samuel Adams when I would have happily written about some dimmer luminary, and for patiently fielding all my neophyte pleas for counsel and assistance. My quick-witted project editor, Megan Schade, provided invaluable comic relief in times of high stress.

Finally, this book would not have been possible without the unfailing love and encouragement of my best friend and partner Alison Rachel Greene, "Of what consequence is it, whether a Turkey is brought on the Table boild or roasted?" Thank you, Alison, so very much.

Benjamin H. Irvin holds degrees from the University of the South, the University of Kentucky College of Law, and Bowling Green State University. He is completing a doctorate in American History at Brandeis University.